ONE SIGNAL
PUBLISHERS
ATRIA

NOT FUNNY

Essays on Life, Comedy, Culture, Et Cetera

JENA FRIEDMAN

ONE SIGNAL
PUBLISHERS

ATRIA

New York • London • Toronto • Sydney • New Delhi

Contents

Prologue

Whenever anyone asks what inspired me to go into comedy, my answer is always the same: 9/11. I know it may not be the most *likable* way to start off, but it's true. Watching people jump to their deaths on live TV just as I was about to enter my first year of college had a traumatizing effect on me and my entire generation. It made me realize that life is short and random and sometimes tragic and that I didn't want to die in a business suit.

Funny stuff, eh?

Growing up in the '90s, I watched a ton of comedy on TV, but the idea of pursuing it as a career never crossed my mind. There were no artists in my family. My parents were always loving and supportive, but thankfully not enough to blunt my comedic edge.

Years ago, at my grandma's funeral, I was comforting my mourning mother when a friend of my grandma's approached us and said, "It's so nice that Freda got to know all her grandchildren as adults."

In her deep state of grief, my mother looked up and without

even missing a beat, she smirked, "Not Jena . . . Jena is not yet an adult." I was twenty-eight years old at the time, living in New York, and bartending to pay the bills because my multiple nightly stand-up shows that paid performers in drink tickets did not provide the most reliable income stream. Since I didn't have a normal, stable job, my mother didn't consider me an "adult." The comment stung, but at least through her immense sadness, my mom could still make people (who weren't her daughter) laugh.

My mom is effortlessly funny, and when I was growing up, she often used humor to cope with life's darkest moments. A lot of the comedy I do today stems from my attempt to do the same: to find levity in tragedy and in doing so, to lighten the mood of anyone listening. It usually works, but sometimes it doesn't, like that time I bombed live on network TV.

I wish I could roll the clip for you now. I looked great. I still had that *the future is female* glow and Rosie the Riveter red NARS lipstick to match. I was even wearing all white for the first time in my life (if you don't count my sister's wedding . . . jk) and dressed like a hipster suffragette.

It was November 8, 2016, and I was in front of a live studio audience (and the world) for *Stephen Colbert's Live Election Night Special.* I was invited to be a guest commentator on Stephen's panel that night, specifically to react in real time to whoever the winner might be.

I almost want to laugh at the naivete of the producer who prepped me for the segment. He had called that morning to go over the format and answer any of my questions. When I demurely asked, "What if Trump wins?" we both laughed nervously.

As a person who had been alive and on Twitter for most of 2016, I had some reservations about the election outcome, but there was so much excitement in the air that morning. Between standing in a line wrapped around an entire city block to vote for our nation's first female president, to the adrenaline rush of preparing for my first *Late Show* appearance, I really didn't want to entertain the thought that Hillary might not win.

Six years earlier I had written for the *Late Show with David Letterman* in the same iconic Ed Sullivan Theater. I had always dreamed of one day being invited on the show as a comedian or as a guest promoting some cool project. Cut to election night, and there I was, living my dream, which was slowly descending into a nightmare as Stephen, the other panelists, and I watched Florida turn red in horror. As it became increasingly clear that an unregistered sex offender was about to become president of the United fucking States of America, the men on the panel seemed surprisingly optimistic, confidently stating that Hillary could still pull through and consoling the crowd with positive aphorisms about the amazing things women have accomplished throughout history. Even as I type this, I can feel a wave of nausea wash over me. In that moment, I was speechless and shocked. I could see the writing on the not-yet-built wall: Trump was going to win.

I didn't know what to do—so I drank a sip of whiskey. I put my head down and inhaled a deep, slow breath.

"Don't cry, don't cry, don't you dare cry in front of your co-workers on live TV," I whispered as I stared at my feet—now purple because my shoes were too small and the theater was too cold (thermal sexism is real). Stephen Colbert, in all his brilliance, kept cool as his panelists unraveled in real time. At one point, Stephen turned to me and asked, "Jena, you're a woman. Everything is on you right now. No pressure."

The audience giggled nervously. "Do you think Hillary can still pull it off? Do you have any hope left?" I was catatonic. I didn't know what to say. I knew the election was over, that our work-in-progress democracy might be over, and that as a "comedian" in that moment, I still had to come up with something funny. So to buy time, I relied on an old TV pundit trick and answered a question with a question: "Do you want my honest answer? Or my TV-friendly answer?"

Stephen's face was hard to read. Up close, I could see a glint of fear in his eyes, but he didn't let the camera pick up on that. He calmly responded, "No, I just want to know how you feel." So I took a deep breath and went for it: "It feels like an asteroid has just crashed into our democracy. It's so sad and heartbreaking and I wish I could be funny—" And then I tried to be funny. "Get your abortions now," I continued to audible audience gasps, "because we're going to be fucked and we're going to have to live with it."

A silence washed over the crowd. I felt so incredibly self-conscious that my line had bombed that, for just a brief moment, my neuroses kicked in and pushed our nation's impending doom into the background. Stephen broke the tension with a joke about CBS's plans to re-air the broadcast later that week. "I don't know what parts are going to be edited out, but I'm pretty sure I've got some idea." The crowd laughed.

I mustered up a smile and tried to brush off my line, realizing comedians on network TV are barely even allowed to say the word "abortion," let alone make a call to action to get one.

The taping ended. I was ushered backstage. I hugged my friends Elna and Molly, who came with me to the show, and they, in turn, hugged Jeff Goldblum (?), who had been a guest on the show earlier that night. I watched some of the male writers break down in tears as Stephen consoled us all. He thanked me for being on the show, which meant a lot, considering I had just alienated almost every Catholic person in his fan base.

The city was eerily quiet when I left the theater that night. I wasn't in New York on 9/11, but people who were often say 11/9 felt similar. The comparisons are notable: both were man-made disasters facilitated by megalomaniacs who used their dad's money to fuck up New York's skyline. I floated stoically through Manhattan that night, in a daze, worried as much about my gaffe as the fate of our country. The next morning, when I spotted a woman carting her infant daughter in a stroller down Seventh Avenue, I broke down and started to cry. That poor woman didn't even need to ask why. She turned to me calmly and said, "It's going to be okay."

In the days that followed, I received more hate mail than I had ever received in my life (though death threats from people who purport to be pro-life do kind of feel like progress?). Worse than the hate mail were the conservative media outlets that picked up my "Get your abortions now" quote and were using it as proof that all pro-choice women were cruel, heartless baby killers. It made me furious that my flippant words could be misconstrued (okay, they were pretty accurately construed) to push a false, destructive narrative and obfuscate the very real threat that Trump's administration posed to reproductive justice and women's health. And although I didn't want to apologize to my critics (a cardinal rule of comedy is "never apologize" . . . in our current era it's also now a cardinal rule of sexual misconduct), I did hold some personal regrets. I wish I had said something softer and less alienating, but equally accurate, like "Get your IUDs now," or "[insert anything funnier]," but I meant what I said, and the facts speak for themselves.

Five years after my late-night gaffe, my too-honest words seem less offensive and less hysterical than when I originally vomited them out of my mouth on live TV because now, more than ever, they ring true. I'll be shocked if *Roe v. Wade* hasn't been overturned by the time you've read this.* Comedy is like that: even when it misfires, there's usually some truth to it. To me, comedy remains the best way to cut through the bullshit, to comfort the grieving, and to change minds, even if it doesn't always make us laugh.

Coming up, you'll read about my unlikely path to becoming a comedian, how I found my voice in an industry, time, and place that for so long seemed so intent on not hearing it, and what it has been like to struggle, survive, and ultimately thrive as a woman in a *comically* unregulated work environment for the past fifteen years.

And at the end of it, if you like what you read, thank Osama bin Laden.

This is *Not Funny*.

---

* . . . fuck. (6/24/22)

Not Funny

"Y ou don't *look* funny. How the hell did you end up being a comedian?"

I get asked this question a lot, and every time I take it as a compliment. The short answer? I failed at every other job I tried.* The long answer is a little more complicated.

Part of the reason I titled this book *Not Funny*† is because it perfectly encapsulates my origin story. It begins my senior year at Northwestern, while I was researching and writing my undergraduate thesis in cultural anthropology. The thesis was called "Whose Truth and Comedy: An Ethnography of Race, Class and Gender in Chicago's Improv Comedy Scene," and it was just as hilarious as it sounds.

The discipline of anthropology has a pretty shady history, involving white men with names like Bronisław and Claude who

---

* Sorry, Mom, I know you wanted me to be a management consultant.
† Good call, Nick.

traveled to remote villages in the farthest corners of the world to "study" the "natives" and then made careers out of writing racist ethnographies about their subjects. I didn't want to go that route, so when it came time to find a topic for my yearlong ethnographic essay—a qualitative research project that involves immersing one-self in a community to observe their behaviors and interactions—I picked a tribe I thought I could blend into easily: female comedians.

I had always been fascinated by comedy, but my left-brained parents would never encourage me to pursue such an unorthodox and unstable profession. In fact, when I finally "came out" to my mother as a comedian, she treated the news like there had been a death in the family. "I'd rather you be gay," she whimpered, "be-cause at least that's something you can't control." She was always the funny one.

At the time I was researching my thesis, I was living in Chicago with three friends who had all studied abroad in various countries the previous year. We built a bond on our life-changing experi-ences overseas (I had spent a semester in Santiago, Chile) and the determination to avoid moving back to our suburban campus, where social life was constructed around the fraternity basement beer-pong circuit. During the summer, we moved into a carriage house in the back of a bar on Halsted and Roscoe, a few blocks from the L train and an easy commute to our classes in Evanston.

Originally, I wanted to write my thesis about female stand-up comedians, but there was a dearth of women in stand-up comedy in Chicago back then and not enough of a sample size for me to study. There was also an improvisational comedy theater a few blocks from where I lived. I had no idea what improv was, but I had always been a sucker for anything within walking distance, and the place was always brimming with activity.

And just like that, I shifted my focus to improv. The site of my ethnography was called ImprovOlympic, later changed to iO after the International Olympic Committee threatened to sue. For a year it was my home—until it wasn't.

You may have heard about iO from alums like Tina Fey, Amy Poehler, Mike Myers, Chris Farley, Tim Meadows, Adam McKay, or countless other famous comedians who have trained there. When I stumbled upon this cult*—I mean "comedy theater and training center"— I had no idea what I was getting into. When I stopped by the place to see how much it would cost to purchase tickets to watch a bunch of shows, the young woman behind the desk—the hilarious Katie Rich, who later went on to write for *Saturday Night Live*—informed me that if I signed up for classes, I could see all the shows for free (that's how they reel you in). I signed up for Level One Improv under the guise of "research," and two months later, I was hooked.

Before improv became a punch line, largely due to the mainstream success of improviser-heavy hit shows like *The Office* and *30 Rock*, Chicago's improv comedy scene was the coolest thing I had ever been part of. The iO classes were full of such interesting and funny students. Many of them had moved to Chicago instead of or right after college to follow their dreams and pursue improv full-time. And my improv teachers were all really kind and encouraging, too. They were obsessed with the art form and always happy to talk to me about it over (many, many) drinks at the theater's bar.

These were also the first adults I had ever met who had been able to make a living (in Chicago, which was an affordable city in 2005) out of teaching and playing what was essentially make

---

* A cult with an even better job placement track record than Scientology!

believe for adults. Coming from my university, where most aspired to investment banking or consulting, this world felt like a much-needed breath of fresh air.

Most fascinating was long-form improv itself, a comedic, physically active art form that at its best evokes the pure, inspirational inventiveness of a jazz ensemble. The creative potential was limitless. You could be your own writer, performer, and director all at the same time. It felt as if a portal to another world had opened, and I never wanted to leave. To this day, I've never experienced as much unbridled joy as I did when creating something out of nothing with my friends and "teammates" onstage at iO.

It's a shame that within a year the same research paper that lured me into this fascinating subculture would be what forced me out of it. My paper had unwittingly amounted to something no private business wants to see: an audit. I looked at this theater-slash-bar-slash-work-environment under a microscope, through a feminist-Marxist lens, and recorded what I found. Obviously, it pissed some people off.

ABSTRACT

Race, gender, and socioeconomic privilege are key elements in the production and consumption of long-form improvisational comedy in Chicago. The bulk of my research includes observations, interviews, and my own experiences performing and working at Chicago's ImprovOlympic Theater and Training Center.

In this essay, I examine how college-educated white women have become a major force in Chicago's improvisational comedy community, on and off the stage. I

analyze the ways in which white women's socialization into
Chicago's improvisational comedy scene differs from that
of nonwhite men and women. I document the experiences
of racially and ethnically marginalized individuals working
in Chicago improv's mainstream to reveal this improvised
comedic performance as a reflection of societal inequalities in
America's urban political economy.

HA HA LOL! I know the paper sounds wonky, and that's because it was. I wasn't a comedian when I wrote my undergraduate
thesis, just an overeager, idealistic college student trying to document an honest account of a lived experience under the guidance
of a radical feminist–Marxist college adviser. We've all done crazy
things in college, right?

Professor Micaela di Leonardo is a rock star in the field of
cultural anthropology. I really wanted to impress her. She was
beloved and equally feared by her students and would often make
essays I turned in hemorrhage with red ink from her critical pen.
I remember during our first class, she told her students about a
pencil-drawing course she once took as a kid that taught her to
draw. She explained that after a few classes, when she would look
at a tree, she wouldn't just see a tree but rather the series of pencil
lines that would enable her to render the tree accurately on paper.
That's also how she explained feminist-Marxist anthropology. By
teaching her students about race, gender, and structural inequality
in certain populations, we would start to see it everywhere. She
was right.

With Professor di Leonardo on board as my thesis adviser, I
wasn't just studying improv; I was looking at the ways in which the
performance of Chicago-style long-form improvisational comedy

and the culture around it reflected a stalled affirmative action agenda in a Bush-era political economy (I know, it's a lot). Translation: Why, after so many decades of "social progress," were these "liberal" spaces still so . . . white? She encouraged me to probe deeper into issues of structural inequality and not hold back when documenting my own enculturation into this magical but flawed subculture. Her teachings had a profound impact on me back then and are still evident in so much of my work to this day.

The thesis was well received, and I even worked toward graduating early from my anthropology program, with honors, so that I could dedicate even more time that spring and summer to my new drug—I mean improv comedy habit.

When a comedy blogger asked to read my thesis, I didn't hesitate to share. *Of course* she could read my little college paper, a dry academic analysis of this comedy institution. What was the worst that could happen?

Man, was I wrong.

Once I gave the blogger permission to post my paper to her site, everyone in our tight-knit comedy scene read it. And because I had disguised my interview subjects' identities through pseudonyms, all the criticism of the "controversial views" expressed throughout my thesis, mostly about racism and sexism I observed at iO, piled onto me.

The fallout was immediate, and in 2005, there was no social media to have my back (I never thought I'd write this, but sometimes social media can be harnessed for good!). Charna Halpern, the owner of the theater, canceled my weekly show from the calendar and kicked me off my improv team. A few days later, two of my favorite former (female) improv teachers called me on the phone and reprimanded me for writing about sexual harassment in my paper rather than keeping it under wraps and reporting it to them directly.

"Women in this community don't make waves offstage," one lectured as I struggled to hold back tears. "We make waves onstage."

I was devastated, and I was confused. I never intended my college paper to make the people I admired and respected most in that scene so angry, or for it to alienate me from a world I had grown to love. Why was it the women in this community—Charna and my two female teachers—who were coming down on me the hardest?* It would take me years to understand why they reacted the way they did, but at the time I felt like I had failed them, that it was I who had done something wrong.

. . .

One specific passage of the forty-three-page thesis seemed to provoke the most outrage. It was a short paragraph where I documented a minor encounter I had as an intern.

> I was reading Barbara Bergmann's *The Economic Emergence of Women*, specifically her chapter on sexual harassment in the workplace, while on my break between performance sets. I was wearing my red and black ImprovOlympic employee T-shirt when a male director and teacher at the theater approached me and initiated conversation by asking me what I was reading. He feigned acknowledgment of the author, grazed my lower back with his hand, and in all seriousness proceeded, "Does your hair naturally flip like that?" When I

---

* Internalized misogyny can be a real bitch.

hesitated to respond, he continued, "Do you know how many women try to make their hair look like that?" I shrugged, laughed uncomfortably at his arbitrary remarks, and continued to read. After three months working at ImprovOlympic, I realized that my socialization offstage was interfering with my ability to "play" onstage. That is, as a female intern I could not repel frequent sexual harassment in the way that I would be expected to—"playing strong"—onstage. I ended my work-study internship prematurely because I had the economic means to pay for classes.

I specifically chose that anecdote to write about *because* it was so benign. I also found humor in the fact that I got lightly harassed while reading about sexual harassment, and I wanted to add some levity to the otherwise heavy subject matter. It's not an easy topic to joke about, people!

But in reality, the harassment I experienced and observed during my internship at that theater was so much more insidious than what I had revealed in my report. Teachers often slept with students and in some cases, gave them stage time in return. Male and female interns were constantly groped and harassed in ways that I didn't find offensive (compared to frat parties) but that I could see how other students might have.

Once when I was working, a male teacher pushed me into a storage closet and asked to feel my arm muscles. I thought it was weird, but I let him. I thought to myself, *At least he asked, right?* Male improvisers were often so handsy and boundaryless with female improvisers onstage that doing so offstage barely registered as inappropriate.

The subtle racism I witnessed at this very white comedy theater was worse. Onstage, white improvisers often tokenized their nonwhite scene partners to milk laughs out of mostly white audiences. Many marginalized students, men and women, ended up leaving the mainstream comedy theaters, like iO and Second City, to form their own separate improv troupes where they wouldn't be subjected to constant racist microaggressions (and macroaggressions) from their mostly white improviser teammates or the mostly white crowds.

For decades, ImprovOlympic had been a pipeline to *Saturday Night Live* as well as many other major comedy career opportunities. If marginalized and underrepresented groups were being pushed out of this community before they ever got a chance to succeed, how did that affect mainstream production of comedy in the larger culture?

A journalist for the *Chicago Reader* reached out to interview me after she heard that backlash to the research paper got me kicked out of iO. I declined her request. I was afraid to speak to her. I didn't want to "make waves offstage" or look like I was trying to get attention. I had already been made to feel like a traitor to a community that had been so welcoming to me, and I didn't want to feel like that again.

I quietly made my exit from iO and looked for ways to get my improv fix elsewhere. For a little while, I performed improv with friends in bars and at smaller, less venerated improv clubs and black-box theaters around Chicago, but it wasn't the same. Nothing could compare to the thrill of performing on a sold-out show on iO's main stage. I still think about how different my career path might have been if I had just kept that paper to anthropology class and never unleashed it into the wilds of Chicago's insular improv comedy community. If I hadn't been blacklisted, maybe I would have eventually gotten more stage time at iO and possibly been invited to perform on one of many highly coveted industry show-cases there. Maybe from there I could have gotten a job writing or performing on *SNL*, and hell, maybe now I'd be . . . probably fired from that hypothetical job at *SNL*. I hear it's a tough place to work.

• • •

Once when I was a student intern at iO, I got an inside tip that Lorne Michaels was on his way to the theater that night to scout for potential cast members; Charna had set up a showcase of her favorite improvisers for him to check out. It was crazy to be a fly on the wall; I can still recall the nervous energy in the room as students crowded on the floor to watch our favorite improv heroes audition for the biggest role of their lives. Some veteran performers barely broke a sweat during their scenes, while others completely choked, all while Lorne sat in stone-faced judgment. While no one ended up getting their big break that night, years later some of my iO friends and heroes—Michael Patrick O'Brien, Vanessa Bayer, Paul Brittain, and Tim Robinson—would get the call to write and perform on *SNL*.

It was heartbreaking to leave that community, and I still get sad thinking about it, but if I hadn't been cast out of my cushy, tight-knit improv bubble, I might never have had the guts to go out on my own. Over the next few years, I focused most of my creative energy on stand-up and sketch writing. The people who had been my friends at iO stayed my friends. After tensions had cooled, I would occasionally stop by the theater to see shows, but I never again performed at the place that I used to consider my second home.

A decade later, I came across an article about women in Chicago's comedy scene fighting back against sexual harassment. The piece was about iO. In 2015 the sexual harassment that I had written about in my college paper had become the subject of multiple articles in mainstream news outlets like Jezebel, BuzzFeed, the *Chicago Reader*, and the *Chicago Tribune*. According to the pieces, iO management had ignored multiple reports of sexual harassment. When one student who had reported her sexual harassment demanded accountability, Charna—still a central figure at the club—offered her free classes. But this time, the student had the power to take the story to social media. Outraged, dozens of other students and former students came forward with their own experiences of sexual harassment at iO and at other comedy theaters in Chicago, New York, and Los Angeles.

Seeing all the press coverage felt vindicating, but it was also frustrating—a decade later, how could this all *still* be going on? Around that time, one of the female iO teachers who had initially reprimanded me when my paper first came out reached out on social media to say hi and to tell me that she was proud of all my success (her words; I will never not have imposter syndrome). She didn't apologize for what she'd said to me years earlier, but she didn't have to. I recognized what she must have been dealing with from her employer or whatever baggage she might have accumulated in her years in the trenches, and I didn't hold it against her. It was also just nice to hear from her.

Comedy, and art in general, is often a step ahead of the culture, and although it was a few years shy of the explosion of the #MeToo movement, after that 2015 sexual harassment shitstorm at iO, some improv comedy clubs around the US finally began to take sexual harassment seriously.

At the Upright Citizens Brigade Theatre in New York, where I performed stand-up regularly, a male performer was kicked out of the community after being credibly accused of rape by multiple women who performed there. The guy ended up suing UCB for reverse gender discrimination (which sounds about right, the rapists always sue), and the court ultimately sided in the comedy club's favor. The landmark ruling echoed throughout the whole community, finally providing a legal framework to make comedy clubs safer for the people who work and perform in those spaces.

At the time I write this, both iO Theaters in Chicago and Los Angeles, the Upright Citizens Brigade Theatres in New York and Los Angeles, and dozens of other performance venues around the country have shuttered in the wake of the Covid-19 pandemic. But I have confidence they'll be back, if nothing else, because cults are a proven and durable business model. And if not those actual theaters, some other incarnation of them will emerge on the scene. And I hope that when they do, the next crop of improv-comedy-theaters-slash-training-centers-slash-bars learn from the mistakes of their predecessors and make their spaces safer and more inclusive, at the very least so that their students can be spared from ever venturing into stand-up.

1,500 Words

Junior year of high school I had an English teacher I'll call Mr. F. Everybody loved Mr. F. He was a towering figure with a deep voice and a permanently furrowed brow. He was tough, exacting, and intimidating. He would push his students to exceed our limits and write outside our comfort zones. Mr. F was eccentric, too. He proved his obsession with *Moby-Dick* through a gnarly tattoo splashed across his forearm. He installed his own set of locks on his classroom door that even the janitors didn't have access to. One time, when my friend showed up to his class with her hair styled differently than she normally wore it, Mr. F snuck up behind her and snipped off a piece of her curl. She didn't report the incident. She, too, loved Mr. F, and she didn't want to get him in trouble.

Mr. F teased a lot of his students, but he rarely messed with me. He had taught my sister four years earlier, and since he was so fond of her and of her entire class (he would rave about them often), he spared me from most of his antics. I was a ball of stress my junior year. I was enrolled in all accelerated classes, prepping for the

SATs, playing three varsity sports, and just trying to make sure I got grades good enough to gain entry to a competitive college from a public high school in New Jersey. Mr. F knew my parents and the pressure they put on me to be a straight-A student. He also lorded that knowledge over me, teasing me about my desire to succeed. "All Friedman cares about is her grades," he would often say, making sure the rest of the class took notice as he mocked me for the audience (as if they were any different).

At the beginning of the year, I averaged a B-minus in Mr. F's class. I read all the assigned books and completed all the coursework as diligently as I could, but I wasn't able to earn above a B on anything. My writing skills had atrophied the previous year, when our English teacher took an extended leave of absence and was replaced by a substitute teacher I can best describe as . . . what's a nice euphemism for dumb? Mr. F would know.

During one class, the substitute teacher lectured us on subliminal bias on standardized tests, like how the word "turquoise" could unintentionally favor privileged kids if students in poorer school districts didn't have the color turquoise in their crayon boxes and therefore didn't know what the word meant (her words, not mine). When the sub asked us to cite examples of subliminal bias that we had come across on standardized tests, I remembered something I had recently seen on a practice verbal SAT test. I raised my hand:

"The analogy 'rower is to regatta' could be elitist because—" Before I could finish the sentence, she interjected, "Right, because inner-city kids don't eat regatta cheese." I cracked a smile, thinking that she was joking. She wasn't.

I don't think I learned anything in that class all year, other than that if all else failed, I could always be a substitute teacher.

By the time I got to Mr. F's class, I hadn't written more than a paragraph in almost a year. I was rusty. Mr. F knew it. Every essay I submitted to him would be returned with snarky notes in the margins. I once wrote a short story inspired by Edward Gorey's *The Hapless Child*, which I thought was dark and funny (and *definitely* on brand) and I was excited for him to read it. The next day Mr. F handed it back to me with one word circled at the top of it: *Trite!* He didn't even bother to correct my spelling or grammar mistakes. As I exited class that day, he called me up to his desk to talk privately. After all the other students had trickled out of the room, Mr. F told me that my writing was unoriginal and that it needed to be more thoughtful and creative if I wanted to succeed.

A big component of Mr. F's class was the personal essay, which also happened to be my Achilles' heel.* When it came to crafting honest prose, I was blocked. When I look back on it, there may have been an "inciting incident," as we call it in screenwriting, contributing to my struggles with the form.

When I was in fifth grade, my mom bought me a diary. It was my least favorite color and motif: pink and floral. It also had a tiny brass lock on it that came with a tiny brass key, so even though I didn't appreciate its aesthetic value, I at least felt confident that whatever I wrote inside that girlie binding would be seen by no one other than me. I wrote everything in that diary. I wrote about how much I hated my sister and what boys I had crushes on. That was everything. I was not that deep at age ten.

I kept the diary hidden under my bed and the key that opened it tucked away in my desk drawer. It was a highly thought-out, foolproof security system, and I trusted that no one would ever be able to penetrate it. I was wrong.

---

* The irony is not lost on me.

One day, my sister found my diary and read it. She was able to pick the lock because she had the strength of ten men, and maybe one scraggly fingernail. She consumed its entire contents in one sitting. Later, when I returned to write in it, I was horrified to see that she had not only picked the lock, but that asshole wrote in it as well. On the page where I mentioned my latest crush, she scribbled that I was stupid and that he would never like me. Even worse, she threatened to tell my crush's older sister, who was on her softball team, my deepest, darkest secret: that I had a romantic interest in her little brother. *Oh, the horror!* I was mortified.

On a side note, my sister and I get along great now. All it took was both of us growing up and moving out of our parents' home. She has no recollection of ever reading my diary, let alone writing such abusive things in it. But I do, and somewhere in a green wood desk drawer in my parents' basement, I have proof.

For the record, years later I did make out with that boy I had a crush on when I was ten, but I never wrote my most intimate thoughts on paper ever again.

Until Mr. F's class.

Every other week, Mr. F would assign students to write journal entries due the following Monday. These entries could be about anything we wanted to write about. The only requirement was that they had to be at least 1,500 words. Mr. F would then read our entries and write notes with copyedits and occasionally life advice in the margins.

I recently found some of my journal entries from Mr. F's class stowed away in a box in the back of a storage closet in my parents' basement. It was a revelation to read them. Twenty years had passed and I had forgotten much of the context around what had inspired each entry. Like the time I almost got arrested for driving my friend Ben's car around a parking lot without a permit. Here's an excerpt from that piece I'd titled "Stupid Sixteen-Year-Old."

As I drove back into the parking lot, I waved to my friends. David mouthed "oh shit" as I turned around and saw two police cars riding my tail. Immediately, I slammed on the brakes. Ben shifted the car into park.

"Switch, Ben," I cried as I jumped on top of him in the passenger's seat. I pushed his scrawny little legs to the driver's side and fastened my seat belt. My body was trembling. As the high beams flashed on us, I knew we were screwed. An officer approached the driver's side window.

"I saw your acrobatic routine." He glanced at me and chuckled. "How old are you?"

"Sixteen," I said timidly.

"Were you driving?" he asked accusingly. Without any time to think, I spoke.

"No, no, I wasn't driving!" He did not believe me. He asked for Ben's license and went back to his car to talk with the other officer. In the car Ben was silent. "Just tell the policeman I was on top of you because," I thought, "well, because we were making out, please! Ben, please tell him you were driving," I begged.

"Jena, lying only gets you into more trouble." I couldn't understand how he could be so calm and cool when I was acting like a spaz . . . [A little later] the officer returned with Ben's license in his hand. He had a smile on his face and sighed.

"I remember the stupid things I did when I was sixteen. Josh (that is the first name on Ben's license), just don't let your girlfriend (I am not his girlfriend) drive the car again." He

peered his head in through the window. "What's your name?"
he asked as he stared at me. "You better tell me."

"Jena Friedman." My eyes filled up with tears as I took a
deep breath.

"You look like you are going to cry," he said.

"We just went around the block once. I'm so sorry. I'm
normally such a good person, really. I'm on the tennis team."
Ben elbowed me and told me to shut up. The officer laughed as
he waved goodbye, got back into his car, and drove away....

I have never in my life felt more privileged than while reading about an encounter I had with a police officer that was so uneventful I had long since forgotten it happened at all. Even now I'm haunted by my innocence at that age and the realization of how differently that night might have gone for Ben and me had we not been white kids from Haddonfield.

In the final paragraph of my entry, I wrote about how lucky I felt that my parents never found out about the events of that night. Mr. F scribbled menacingly in the margins, *Maybe I'll blackmail you*. He always wrote wry, provocative remarks like that. I knew he was joking and that my secret would be safe with him. He gave me a B, mostly because of my grammatical errors, and advised me to be "more reflective and less narrative" next time.

Mr. F wanted me to write "more personal" essays. I wanted to get an A in his class. After reading the same note week after week, I decided to give in and write something more personal with the hope that Mr. F might like it. In my next essay, I shared details about a party I went to over the weekend and the name of the boy I kissed at it. I wondered why I was even attracted to a guy who "doesn't take showers and has drunk pee before." When Mr. F returned the essay, it had a large pencil check mark at the top of it, and my first B-plus. "Quite a revealing journal entry," he wrote on the last page. "I'd like to talk with you. Today."

I don't remember what we talked about that day, but getting above a B on a journal entry in Mr. F's class was a revelation. Had I finally broken through? Were my writing skills finally rising to Mr. F's near-impossible standards? As I continued to overshare details of my nascent personal life in these weekly essays, my grades in Mr. F's class steadily improved.

It didn't occur to me that my teacher's interest in the social lives of teenagers was a bit odd, or that it was strange to reward me with good grades for divulging details about mine. After all, this was creative writing. Art knows no boundaries! For the first time in my life, I was writing something that an adult found interesting, and it felt pretty cool. Mr. F started showing up to watch my tennis matches after school, too. Neither my mom (who was always in attendance) nor I thought anything about it. Mr. F followed all the high school sports and was close with a lot of his students.

• • •

Six years later, a student in my sister's class wrote an op-ed in a national newspaper about a toxic, traumatic affair she had had with a married, middle-aged high school teacher when she was just seventeen years old. That teacher was Mr. F.

When I found out, all I could think about was how easy it must have been for him to target and groom her, given how much unbridled access he had to all his students' private thoughts, which he teased out of us in those journal entries. I had always gotten a vibe that Mr. F was a little creepy (he would be the first to admit it), but

I had no idea he could be so reckless, destructive, and—what's the word I'm looking for?—trite!

Okay, "trite" might not be the right word choice (Mr. F, again, would know), but the predatory teacher/mentor trope is so infuriatingly unoriginal. It's a tired, pervasive cliché that causes trauma in its victims and extinguishes so much potential in its wake. If only Mr. F had been as responsible in his actions as he encouraged all his students to be in our writing . . . but he wasn't.

Mr. F has since passed away, but I still think of him and the influence he had on my writing. The memories are complicated. The guy who used his power to manipulate underage students was also the guy who first taught me how to write personal essays.

Maybe that's why after all these years I'm still more comfortable with one-liners.

An American Girl's Story

In 2006 I was invited to write on a political sketch show at a hole-in-the-wall comedy theater in Chicago. *Cappin' the Week* was in the vein of *The Daily Show*, only unpaid and less funny. I was new to sketch writing and thrilled at the opportunity to write and perform for a live, paying audience of actual people (rather than just other comedian friends).

The first sketch I pitched was a darkly comedic piece about date rape. The joke was that instead of saying the word "rape," the character in the scene said the word "duke" in its place. This was around the time of the Duke lacrosse scandal, and I thought "date duke" might catch on as a clever euphemism. (Spoiler alert: it didn't.) That sketch was as awkward and unfunny as it sounds, and I don't think it even made it past the table read.

My first piece that finally did end up in the show was inspired by recent reports of avian flu circulating in Vietnam and Thailand and my fear that it might soon turn into a global pandemic (I was always ahead of my time when it came to airborne pathogens). But unlike the subject matter, my bird flu material didn't exactly kill (sorry for the pun). After a few more false starts, I hit my stride in week three when I found my muse: American Girl.

To the uninitiated, American Girl, Inc. is an educational toy doll company that began as a way to teach children about the past by selling historically themed dolls with accompanying books. But by the mid-2000s, the once modest doll shop founded by a retired teacher, Pleasant Rowland, had sold out to Mattel and morphed into a multimillion-dollar brand.

In 2005 American Girl had come under fire for their Doll of the Year, Marisol Luna, the collection's first Mexican American girl. What sparked outrage was Marisol's backstory, the folksy origin tale that comes printed in each $100-plus toy doll's book. Marisol's was about how she fled her "dangerous" Chicago neighborhood of Pilsen and moved to the "sleepy Chicago suburb of Downers Grove." Naturally, many residents of this proud, working-class Mexican American enclave (and home to the National Museum of Mexican Art, no less) did not appreciate their community's portrayal in Marisol's origin story. Outraged protesters even showed up at American Girl Place, the doll company's flagship location on the Magnificent Mile, to express their complaints.

I had never been into the dolls as a kid (I was a cool kid), but after reading about the Marisol Luna controversy in the *Chicago Tribune*, I became obsessed. If the corporate behemoth was so clueless in their rollout of Marisol, surely they must have other blind spots I could exploit for comedic purposes! I stopped by AGP one afternoon to investigate.

As I walked into the store, with the color palette of a Caucasian vagina, I was greeted by a cacophony of gleeful shrieks.

Little girls of all shapes and sizes of white privilege ran around clutching their ratty, abused dolls in one hand and any accessories they could grasp in the other. There was a restaurant that hosted tween birthday parties and featured a menu of overpriced finger foods, mocktails, and actual alcohol to sedate frazzled adult guardians. There was a doll hospital, where even the most sadistic girls could have their dolls patched up for free, and a theater where you could buy thirty-four-dollar tickets to see an hour-long "musical," more accurately described as a melodic sales pitch for the entire American Girl collection. Of course I went to see it. (Twice.)

And what a collection it was! My favorite doll was Kit Kittredge, a Depression-era girl who could be equipped with over $1,000 in accessories. Even her toy broom cost more than a real one. Then there was Addy Walker, the one Black doll in the bunch, whose backstory was that she was a runaway slave. So nuanced! And who could forget Samantha Parkington, the OG American Girl, who protested child labor. I learned about her backstory from the musical. The real-life child actress who played Samantha gave a truly memorable performance during the show, which was just one of twenty-two shows that ran each week. Oh, and I later learned the actress who played the doll protesting child labor was herself an overworked, underpaid, underage non-union worker.* You can't make this stuff up.

It was a comedy writer's gold mine. Not just a place to buy dolls, but rather a whole experience built on selling a white-

---

* According to a 2006 article in the *New York Times*, the adult actors in the show tried to join AFTRA, but they failed, and eventually American Girl Place just stopped putting on shows.

washed, pseudo-inclusive ethos to any parents willing to pay for it. I knew I had to poke fun at this cultural snake pit, but how? I decided to borrow a page from the Garbage Pail Kids and create a fictionalized doll company of my own.

Enter Refugee Girl. Instead of the gross-out humor signature to Garbage Pail Kids, I leaned into the inherent tone deafness of the American Girl universe to inspire my work. I imagined a world in which all the most insane aspects of this enterprise—the whitewashing of history, the commoditization of real girls' experiences, and the hefty price tags—were magnified to reveal just how fucked-up this faux-feminist institution was. I pitched the idea to my sketch group a few days later, and next thing I knew, I was given a weekly five-minute block in the live show to test out my American Girl parody.

My first character was Fallujah Jones, an Iraq war refugee "with a strong spirit and survival instincts" (they all had that), who fled to America after the US military attacked her Baghdad elementary school playground in search of terrorists believed to have set up shop in the jungle gym. In the sketch, Fallujah was marketed to a little girl in the Chicago suburb of Peoria, who could learn about "Western neo-imperialism from the safety and comfort of her pink-and-white Laura Ashley bedroom." When I performed it to the (possibly inebriated) late-night crowd of political comedy junkies, they ate it up.

For the next few weeks, I wrote and performed a series of sketches, each featuring a different Refugee Girl. There was Bahati Smith, a Darfur refugee who came to America after a Hollywood movie star adopted her and brought her to the States; Guadalupe Hidalgo Flores, an undocumented laborer for Liz Claiborne in Plano, Texas, who crawled to America through a rat-infested drainage tunnel (her story was largely inspired by the 1983 Gregory Nava drama *El Norte*). And who could forget Payne Gone, a 2004 Indonesian tsunami refugee, who rode the wave all the way to a new life in America!

The comedy teetered on the precipice of what might now be considered problematic, but to me the satire was clear: the target was never the fictional refugees, but rather the doll company exploiting their harrowing tales of survival for profit.

By show eight, I had enough lovable characters with oversimplified backstories to fill a whole play, so I did exactly that. In a matter of a few caffeine-fueled weeks at coffee shops around Chicago, my musical comedy *The Refugee Girls Revue* was born.

The script closely mirrored the original show: *The American Girls Revue*. The plot of that show was simple: a new girl moves to town and joins the American Girls Club, where a group of tweens gather every week to act out their favorite American Girl dolls' stories. In my parody, Katrina and her little sister Rita are poor, Black, orphaned IDPs (internally displaced people) from New Orleans who are resettled to a predominantly white, upper-middle-class suburb. There, a club of oblivious, privileged tweens teach the traumatized IDPs "what it's like to be a *real* refugee girl" by acting out their favorite refugee girl dolls' stories. It was pretty edgy even for 2007, but I had a community of brilliant comedian friends who I knew would be able to help me pull it off.

I must have been glowing when I finished the first draft of the script, because the moment I closed my laptop, an elderly man with a shamanic vibe (he was wearing a shawl indoors) approached me without introduction. He simply came up and whispered, "You look like you just gave birth." Now, I had gained a few pounds since moving from the East Coast to the Midwest, but apparently that's not what he meant as he continued, "To an idea."

"Oh. Okay." I hadn't seen that coming. Was this just his standard pickup line? When he asked to sit down, I cautiously indulged him. He seemed harmless enough, and even if he was a serial killer, it would probably have been hard for him to murder me in a crowded coffee shop in broad daylight.

"Where do you think the most fertile place in the world is?"

I had no idea, so I said the first thing that came to mind. "The Fertile Crescent in Mesopotamia?"

He paused for dramatic effect.

"Cemeteries!" he exclaimed. "Because that's where dreams go to die. So many people don't have the guts to live their dreams, so when they die, their dreams get buried with them and leak into the soil. That's why cemeteries are always so green and full of life." Wow. I was not expecting that. I'm not sure the logic tracked, but his theory shook me to my core. It also gave me goose bumps.

Before I could respond, the man just got up AND WALKED AWAY. He didn't even turn back to say goodbye. I looked around to make sure other people had seen him, too, that he wasn't some apparition I had just imagined. It didn't matter—that brief encounter was all I needed to hear to do whatever it would take to get my script off the ground.

The Refugee Girls Revue was the first play that I ever wrote and produced. It was also the only play that I ever wrote and produced, because once you put up a play, with an eleven-person ensemble cast, on your own dime, with no prior experience in theater production or any financial backing, you never do something so stupid again. It was an insane undertaking that I was only able to pull off with the aid of a talented and dedicated cast and crew of comedian

friends who all volunteered their time, for free (!!), to help me actualize my crazy, grandiose vision.

Over the next month, my cast rehearsed multiple times a week
at a free space in Boystown* as I worked behind the scenes to pro-
cure a venue for the play's limited run. All the improv clubs were
booked for months (or so they told me), so I landed on an eight-
week slot at the Apollo (not *that* Apollo), a small, independent theater in Lincoln Park. I had never put up a show before, anywhere,
let alone in a major city, and I couldn't grasp how in-over-my-head
I truly was, but my cast's belief in me and in the project buoyed me
whenever my self-doubt crept in.

Soon it was opening night, which went surprisingly well! No
one in the cast forgot their lines. My skeleton crew (by "crew" I
mean a stage manager and the theater's lighting designer) didn't
fumble once on lighting or sound cues. And the audience laughed
in all the right spots. What a relief! We did it! We actually pulled
off a pretty good show! For the next two days, I was on cloud nine;
that is, until I read our first review in *Time Out Chicago*.

THE REFUGEE GIRLS REVUE (one star)

Misconceived, amateurish musical satire . . . The attempts at
comedy are . . . flat-footed, with most ranging from the unending
hilarity of calling another girl "bitch" to the none-too-subtle political
jabs. . . . [Friedman's] staging achieves a level of polish usually
reserved for a summer camp talent show. If that amateurish quality
is intentional, it still needs a certain degree of sophistication,
something this cast and crew have failed to muster. —Kay Daly

---

*Thank you, Marc Rubin's gallery.

To this day, that remains one of the worst reviews I have ever read, let alone received. I wasn't sure I wanted to include it in this book, because even reading it now still evokes a mild PTSD. There's so much I want to say about it, too. Like that it misquotes us numerous times. The play had its faults, but it also had punch lines.

To make matters worse, *Time Out Chicago*'s comedy editor, a guy I knew socially from the city's stand-up circuit, dragged my cast in the weekly listings, too, writing, "With such a talented cast [...] we're surprised they ever let this happen." He also later called my show "The Worst Comedic Attempt of 2007," in the end-of-the-year issue, which is kind of funny, because "Worst Comedic Attempt" WASN'T EVEN A CATEGORY in the magazine in prior years. Apparently, it had been created specifically for *me*, so that's something.

I was so embarrassed and depressed after that asshole-ripping write-up. I stayed in bed for a whole week, until I had to get out of bed the following Saturday to rally my demoralized team for that night's show, which went about as well as you can expect. One of my cast members was so stressed about our awful review that she dropped out of the run and I (having ZERO musical theater chops) had to fill in for her until I found a replacement. On a side note, I really wish I had gotten that night's show on tape.

As I kept putting out small fires to keep the show going, that one-star review kept weighing on me. Was the reviewer right? Was the show overly preachy? Did we really miss the mark?

But in spite of the bad press, the cast persisted and found joy in performing with each other and accomplishing what we had set out to do in the first place: make an edgy, relevant political satire and have fun in the process. Also, surprisingly, thanks to word of mouth, audiences kept showing up. By the end of the run, I had broken even on my production costs and we were actually selling out, mostly to audiences of teen girls, including quite a few former actresses from the original American Girl production.

After our eighth week, with little fanfare, our show ended. I put my dreams of working in comedy on the back burner and got a job as a copywriter at a graphic design firm in downtown Chicago to pay the bills. A few months later, I had almost forgotten that I submitted the script to the New York International Fringe Festival until I received a letter in the mail informing me that *The Refugee Girls Revue* had been accepted into the festival. I had pretty much given up on the show by that point, but a chance to perform it in New York City was a dream. Would my beleaguered cast actually be up for it after everything we had been through?

A few nights later, I called us all together (the ones who were still speaking to me) and soft-pitched the idea. To my surprise, everyone wanted to do it. We agreed that this time, I would bring on an actual theater director to help steer the ship. One of the actors recommended a grad student in directing whom she loved and thought we could possibly convince to direct the show.

When I met with the director, Scott Illingworth, I liked him immediately. He also didn't need any convincing! He understood exactly what I was trying to convey with the script and helped me hone the satire and polish the choreography so that our "summer camp talent show" aesthetic would come across as more deliberate. I also made one key revision: a complete overhaul of the final song.

Originally, our show ended in a fourth-wall-breaking song/plea to encourage our audience to donate to local refugee resettlement organizations: "We know this play may be a buzzkill, but donate to these local nonprofits," my cast of comedians belted as they handed out flyers about local refugee organizations (who we had partnered with) to the crowd. So maybe it was a little overly preachy.

In the updated version, with the help of my friend—and incredibly talented musician—Elia Einhorn, I cut the preachy, fundraising aspect of the final song and instead leaned in to the slick, consumer catnip vibe I was parodying. The new finale featured an upbeat jingle, a last-ditch sales pitch to audiences to purchase a doll from the Refugee Girl collection. During the curtain call, each actress would appear center stage, waving goodbye as she held up a sign that read BUY in her character's native language. It was a perfect satirical ending to a satirical show.

When we debuted this slightly revised version of *The Refugee Girls Revue* at the New York International Fringe Festival, I mentally prepared myself for disappointing reviews. The day after our opening night I picked up a copy of *Time Out New York* and nervously flipped to the theater section.

TIME OUT NEW YORK

THE REFUGEE GIRLS REVUE (four stars)

Nothing is safe or sacred in this deliciously wicked spoof that is *The Refugee Girls Revue*. . . . As smart as it is amusing, *The Refugee Girls Revue* uses off-color humor to suggest that, although we're no longer living in a time of cholera, our dolls (and we) still have a hell of a lot to endure. —Amanda Waas

I felt truly vindicated. Finally, someone got it! I was so proud of my cast for sticking with the show and relieved that I hadn't let them down. New York critics seemed to have a completely different view on things. The feedback on our show was *so* positive, in fact, that it caused me to rethink my career trajectory entirely. Maybe there was something more the comedy world had in store for me beyond writing for free at a weekly sketch show and having my work be eviscerated by a failed stand-up comic turned comedy editor at a magazine back in Chicago.

By the end of my show's brief Fringe Festival run, I decided to pack my bags and move to New York City that summer for good.

Years later, a comedian would tell me, "You're never a prophet in your homeland." We were talking about her experience working with what at the time was a little-known sketch group called the Upright Citizens Brigade in Chicago. (Okay, fine, it was Amy Poehler. Sorry to name-drop, but it's the best name to drop!) Amy shared that she found mainstream success after she left Chicago, and that so much of the Chicago politics she dealt with in her early years ultimately fell away when she and the rest of the UCB found their tribe in New York City. And I would, too.

I'm technically from New Jersey, but as a young adult I considered Chicago my comedy homeland. It was where I fell in love with writing and performing comedy, and where I discovered my early comedy heroes who inspired me. For three years, I performed stand-up, improv, and sketch comedy almost every night, multiple times a night, and worked tirelessly to get any traction there that could bring me closer to a coveted paid gig in comedy. Yet after a blacklisting from iO and then having my first show labeled THE WORST COMEDIC ATTEMPT OF 2007 in *Time Out Chicago*, I was at a crossroads and close to quitting.

It was only in New York that things really started to come together for me—I met so many comedians who made their livings doing comedy and who would later become friends and mentors, I got a manager and started submitting packets to write for late night, and eventually got one of those coveted writing jobs—but in the process I hadn't changed much about myself or my work ethic. It was my community, the new opportunities, and my sense of what was possible that had shifted.

I had needed to strike out on my own first, to accept that big risk of failure, to give me the strength to weather any future ups and downs in my unpredictable, frankly insane industry. Like great American heroines Marisol Luna and Kit Kittredge before me, leaving home was what I'd needed to discover who I really was all along! Okay, fine, that last sentence may have been a little shoehorned in, but I think you get where I'm going with this. . . .

Jena Friedman™: An American Girl

Hilary Fitzgerald Campbell

Meet Jena: an American girl who grew up in a small town outside of Philly (okay, fine, New Jersey) in the 1990s during the most prosperous era in American history. As a child, Jena dreamed of someday moving to the big city to become a writer/performer/multi-hyphenate, but her left-brained, neurotic parents feared unorthodox career paths and discouraged her creative impulses. When Jena wanted to join her high school's drama club, her loving but critical mother said "tough shit" and made her sign up for winter track instead. Jena's parents worried about their daughter's future and didn't want her to grow up to become a "drug-addicted starving artist," not even aware of how expensive drugs can be or that not all "starving artists" even do drugs.

Our story begins on September 11, 2001, just as Jena is about to enter her first year of college (ruh-roh). You can guess what happened next, as it's probably a little too dark for a children's story. In any event, what transpired on 9/11 scarred Jena for life and made her determined to do whatever it would take not to die in a business suit! (Hence, her budding interest in comedy.)

In *Let's Get a Real Job*, follow Jena as she convinces her mom that she'll be able to find a real job with a BA in cultural anthropology and then lands a coveted gig in health-care consulting at a global management consulting firm, where Jena learns to "deliver innovative solutions that endure" or whatever it said on the company pen. Jena sucked at that job and left soon after, but it taught her many valuable life lessons: like "fake it till you make it," and "don't order sushi for you and your colleagues in midtown Manhattan after midnight."

In *Jena Gets Her Ass Handed to Her*, explore the pitfalls of independent theater production and small-town politics as Jena gets her ass handed to her while trying to put up a play on a shoestring budget in a myopic comedy town.

In *Rock Bottom*, read about that time Jena struggled to make ends meet while working three jobs simultaneously in New York City, which culminated in one fateful night where she fainted and broke three teeth after smoking pot on an empty stomach in the basement of the Bowery Poetry Club. It's a cautionary tale, but a necessary one.

Throughout all of Jena's misadventures, she discovers that while she can't always control the world around her, she can control how she reacts to it. Jena's stories show how to face challenges head-on with perseverance, determination, and most importantly, humor.

This character set includes:

A mini health insurance card, the most important accessory for any freelance comedian, even if it doesn't cover dental

A $22 notebook* that you too can write jokes in that hopefully won't get you in trouble

A bottle of cold-brew iced coffee and Oatly oat milk, which is Jena's primary addiction, since marijuana doesn't exactly agree with her (see *Rock Bottom*)

A $600 toy iPhone, made by kids in China,† that you can actually tweet from, but be careful!

---

* The same notebook is available for three dollars at CVS.
† Just like the real iPhone used to be!

Dead Baby Jokes, or,

How to Talk to a Fetus Lawyer

Why do you put a baby in a blender feetfirst?
To see the expression on its face.
—ARISTOPHANES

Hear me out.

For as long as I can remember, I've been obsessed with dead baby jokes. They're dark and fucked-up and they kill almost every time, assuming they're told in a room without any visibly pregnant people. They also hold attention. They can shock and awe and shift conversation away from any other topic hanging over the atmosphere of the room. But once you tell one, you have to own it, because after the dead baby (joke) is out of the bottle, there's no going back. Let me show you what I mean.

A woman is giving birth. The doctor delivers the baby and says, "Congratulations! You have a healthy baby boy." The

43

woman cries tears of joy and reaches for her child. Instead of handing it to her, the doctor takes the baby by the ankle and swings it around the room. The mother shrieks. The doctor continues to toss the baby around as if it's pizza dough. At one point, the doctor throws the baby into the ceiling fan, little baby limbs get tangled into the blades, and little baby parts splatter all over the walls.* All the while, the poor new mom screams, "What are you doing to my baby?" The doctor gives the baby back to the mom and says, "April Fool's. It was already dead."

Yikes. Are you okay? Uncomfortable? Want me to change the subject? Too bad, I can't now. And that's another reason why dead baby jokes are so incredibly effective: they steal focus.

Dead baby jokes can also be deployed as tools for subterfuge. As a preteen, I often relied on DBJs to distract my peers from their more insidious attempts at humor. In middle school, some of my classmates often entertained each other with racist and anti-Semitic jokes. "Why did the Polish guy cross the road?" I don't know, it's really none of my business. "How many Jews does it take to screw in a light bulb?" As the only Jewish kid at the table, I was afraid to find out. There were far worse jokes that I'd rather not give the honor of appearing in print, but you get the gist. Since I didn't "look Jewish" (whatever that means), I regularly found myself as a fly on the wall for middle school shock-comic open-mic sessions my non-passing friends weren't privy to.

It always made me uncomfortable to hear kids tell such bigoted

---

*I added this line for dramatic effect. Dead baby jokes encourage artistic license.

jokes, but I never said anything because I was young and insecure and afraid their ire would turn on me. So when I wanted to change the subject, I would just whip out a dead baby joke to stun everyone around me into silence.

Since there are dead babies of every race, creed, culture, religion, and income bracket, jokes about them are equal opportunity offenders. A well-placed dead baby joke can trump any racist, sexist, anti-Semitic, or homophobic barb (see what I did there?) and push the humor to a perhaps creepy—but fortunately *inclusive*—place.

DBJs also encourage creativity. They are jokes on training wheels. The structure is so simple that the punch lines write themselves. In your typical dead baby joke, the opening sentence is so shocking and disturbing that all you have to do for the second half to work is simply let out the tension. Case in point:

Why do you put a baby in a blender feetfirst?

Don't think about it for too long; really any response will do. The original "So you can see the expression on its face" is clever, but wittiness is not even a requirement with these morbid little zingers. "Why not?" also works as a punch line, as does the pragmatic answer, "Because it doesn't fit headfirst." It took me two seconds to come up with that. The paint-by-numbers nature of these jokes makes an otherwise esoteric concept like joke writing something any aspiring comedian, attention-seeking kid, or total psychopath can wrap their head around.

On a side note, I'm glad you're still with me.

According to the academic journal *Western Folklore*, dead baby jokes were first born in the late 1800s United Kingdom, because

Seth Olenick

of course they were. If you've never consumed British, Scottish, Welsh, or Northern Irish comedy, you're missing out. It's dark as fuck. I have always attributed their penchant for gallows humor to the fact that the countries that make up the UK are so . . . old. They have survived and reckoned with centuries of terror—often self-generated, but terror nonetheless—and trauma. Whereas we in the US have just buried it.

Unsurprisingly, my stand-up goes over pretty well whenever I perform over there.

In 1899 English poet Harry Graham wrote the first documented dead baby poem:

> *Willie with a thirst for gore*
> *Nailed the baby to the door.*
> *Mother said with humor quaint,*
> *Willie dear, don't spoil the paint.*

Notice how even from its very inception, dead baby humor was, dare I say, feminist! In just a few lines, the poet depicts a female character who is so multifaceted. She's a nurturing mother, a paint connoisseur, and an accessory to child abuse, and, unlike the baby in the poem, you can't pin her down.

I have no idea where I heard my first dead baby joke, probably on a camp bus or from some savvy, older neighborhood kid (the original Twitter). According to American folklorist Alan Dundes, dead baby jokes first appeared in the US in the 1960s and '70s. Dundes attributed the popularity of these jokes to the war in Vietnam and the general cultural upheaval of the era, writing in 1979 that "the dead baby joke cycle is a reflection of American culture . . . if anything is sick, it is the society that produces the sick humor."[*]

I don't consider dead baby jokes a by-product of a sick society. Rather, like so much of the art and music of the 1960s and '70s (including disco!), they're a reflection of a traumatized society trying to heal itself through culture. It's not surprising that dead baby jokes flourished in America in the 1970s. As women were fighting for equal rights and reproductive autonomy, perhaps dead baby jokes acted as a pressure valve to alleviate anxieties around motherhood as well as social stigmas associated with abortion.

As edgy and provocative as dead baby jokes may sound, they're also completely innocuous. Unlike racist jokes, which can serve to normalize prejudicial views, there's no danger in telling a joke about some hypothetical baby in a blender. If countless studies have shown that violent video games don't harm kids,[†] I can't imagine morbid, equal-opportunity one-liners do, either. If anything, joking about a dead baby is far better for society than joking about a live one, and by a live baby, I mean Donald Trump.

It may seem like a stretch to link dead baby jokes to live baby ex-presidents (I'm writing this pre-2024 . . . who knows what the future will bring), but not when you consider the role humor

---

[*] Alan Dundes, "The Dead Baby Joke Cycle," *Western Folklore* 38, no. 3 (1979): 145–57.

[†] Alex Hern, "Playing Video Games Doesn't Lead to Violent Behavior, Study Shows," *Guardian*, July 21, 2020.

played in catapulting Trump into the White House in 2016. Many scholars of Internet culture* have theorized that part of what pushed Trumpism into the mainstream was that his presidential run started out as a bad joke on social media.

In the years leading up to the 2016 election, kids were priming themselves for our tangerine-toned nightmare out in the darkest corners of the internet, on sites like 4chan and 8chan, shocking each other with the most inappropriate, fucked-up jokes they could find. Not so different from what my friends and I used to do IRL in the '90s, but in a digital environment, the available content was so much more dangerous and depraved than anything we were ever exposed to as kids. When my friends and I would sit around a table trying to out-shock each other with offensive jokes, there weren't random adults sitting there with us. But online, kids and adults comingle, and in the darkest corners of the internet, a lot of those adults are actual Nazis!

And in the internet era, on so many online message boards, powerful algorithms encouraged and amplified the most deplorable, clickable content. If I had written a dead baby joke in an online chat room circa 2014, it never would have gotten any traction, let alone distracted anyone away from the racist, anti-Semitic humor that was spreading like wildfire. If anything, my dead baby jokes would have just been down-voted or ignored.

Honestly, it's a shame, when you think about it: Where might we be now if more kids online had been able to use dead baby jokes to steer their peers away from getting sucked down racist, fascist rabbit holes?

In this current moment of cultural upheaval, where our nation

---

* Can I cite myself as a source here?

is so fractured and polarized, I see a clear opening for the kind of dark, absurdist comedy that only dead baby jokes can provide. DBJs unify; they bring people together, in laughter *and* in disgust. Dead baby jokes are democratic: they work well in almost any audience (maybe not a maternity ward or a pro-life rally).

Dead baby jokes are inclusive, inspirational, tension-breaking, and maybe even healing. Yes, that's right, dead baby jokes are . . . healing. Because what's funnier than a dead baby?

A. *A dead baby in a clown costume*
B. *Two dead babies*
C. *Depends on what you find funny*
D. *All of the above*

• • •

Abortion jokes are dead baby jokes for adults. They're equally shocking, but way more pointed and political (because women's personal decisions are apparently political). Joan Rivers joked about abortion before the procedure was even legal in the US, and female comics have been following in her footsteps ever since. In one of Joan's early bits, she joked about how friends of hers would leave the country to get "appendectomies," a euphemism everyone in her audience understood and laughed at. She explained further in a later interview with NPR, "By making jokes about it [abortion], you brought it into a position where you can look at it and deal with it . . . and take control of it."*

---

*Joan Rivers, interview by Terry Gross, "Comedian Joan Rivers Is a Real 'Piece of Work,'" *Fresh Air*, NPR, June 9, 2010, https://www.npr.org/transcripts/127556307.

When I first got into stand-up, the textbook dead baby jokes I had told as a kid served as a blueprint for the more personal, original dead baby jokes that I would write and perform as an adult. It just so happened that many of those jokes would veer into the political minefield that is abortion. Abortion's seat at the proverbial table of cultural currency, that it is so taboo and yet also so universal,* makes it perfect fodder for comedic excavation.

My first abortion joke was inspired by a real experience I had with a friend and her gynecologist (this setup is already a little too on the nose). We all met up for drinks and by the end of the night, the gynecologist got wasted and then drunk-drove her car home.† The next day, she called me to see if I wanted to be her patient. I didn't know how to respond, so I politely declined and came up with a joke about it instead. It wrote itself.

A drunk-driving gynecologist? How can I trust someone who makes such poor life decisions . . . to help me get rid of mine?

By my mid-twenties, I had written so many abortion jokes, the sheer number of them in my comedic arsenal became a joke in itself.

I have a lot of abortion jokes. The best thing about abortion jokes is that no one tries to steal them. They're like the unwanted children of jokes.

---

* According to a news release from the Guttmacher Institute on October 19, 2017, nearly one in four women in the US will have an abortion by age forty-five. Gutmacher Institute, "Abortion Is a Common Experience for U.S. Women, Despite Dramatic Declines in Rates," news release, October 19, 2017, https://www.guttmacher.org/news-release/2017/abortion-common -experience-us-women-despite-dramatic-declines-rates.

† We tried to stop her!

Today abortion jokes are a staple in so many female comics' acts, and not just because they kill every time (I couldn't resist) or for the shock value they provide, but because the laws around women's health in the US and abroad are still so absurd and unjust that if we couldn't find a way to laugh about it, we'd probably just cry.

In 2012 I read about legislation in Virginia that required women in need of abortions to look at ultrasound images of their fetus before they were eligible to obtain the procedure in the state. The law was cruel, unnecessary, and not backed by science. I wanted people outside the realm of abortion activism to know just how absurd this paternalistic law looked in the real world, where it served only to make it harder for women to receive medical care. So I wrote a joke about it.

> If you want to get an abortion in Virginia, they first make you get an ultrasound, where they show you a photo of the fetus and then they send you away to deliberate on it for twenty-four hours or forty-eight or seventy-two . . . or until it's crowning.
>
> Where's the science that says that showing me a photo of my fetus is going to make me want to keep it? They're not cuddly. Republican lawmakers, if you want me to keep a child, I respect your choice not to respect mine, but at least sell me on it. Don't show me a photo of a fetus, show me a photo of something that resonates, like, I don't know, a photo of myself in sixty years, trying to walk down a flight of stairs alone.

Unlike dead baby jokes, which merely offend (sometimes), abortion jokes are threatening. They attack the inherent power imbalances in our society and, because they're political (the personal is political when it comes to anyone who's not a white dude), undermine the status quo. The early 2000s, when I first got into comedy, saw abortion rights under steady assault from the right. Joking about abortion felt as relevant as I imagine it felt for my second-wave feminist heroes of the 1970s. But if a tree falls in the woods and no one is around to hear it, does it really make a sound? That's how I felt about my abortion material at the time. And I was not alone—so many female comedians were telling abortion jokes at open mics and in comedy clubs across the country, but few ever made it on TV—I'm talking about the abortion jokes *and* the female comedians.

In 2011 I was hired to write for the *Late Show with David Letterman*. I got the job because of a packet I submitted that contained zero abortion jokes. If you're curious, here are a few of the jokes that I did submit. Heads up: they're a little dated.

Top Ten Rejected Prom Themes

10. *"16 and Pregnant"*
 9. *"Newark, Newark"*
 8. *"Saturday Night Fever Blister"*
 7. *"Springtime in Paris, Texas"*
 6. *No Prom—High School Gym Taken Over by FEMA*
 5. *"Romeo and Giuliani"*
 4. *"Under the Sea, sponsored by the good people at British Petroleum"*
 3. *"Lady in Red . . . for president in 2012"*
 2. *"Jihad the Time of My Life"*
 1. *"Unforgettable-ish"*

Top Ten Questions on the Application to Replace Osama bin Laden

10. Tell us about your last jihad.
9. How did you hear about Al Qaeda?
8. Do you work well under pressure?
7. If you could bomb any embassy in the world, which would it be and why?
6. Have you taken any on-camera classes?
5. Tell us about a time you planned a suicide mission from start to finish.
4. Are you willing to relocate?
3. How many counterfeit rupees can fit inside this cave?
2. What is your expected starting salary—in terms of nuclear weapons?
1. Would you take the job for seventy-one virgins?

Top Ten Signs There's Already Trouble in the William and Kate Marriage

10. They've changed their Facebook status to "it's complicated."
9. They ride on different levels of the double-decker bus.
8. Will's been spending more time watching football— American football.
7. Kate's been "too tired" to touch the crown jewels.
6. Will's been taking really long showers.
5. Kate stopped dispelling rumors that she's Jewish.

4. *Will got caught tweeting strange women pictures of his deal.*

3. *Kate's new nickname for Will is "Not So Big Ben."*

2. *Will's new nickname for Kate is "Pippa."*

1. *They're acting cold and distant—even for British people.*

See! I can be funny when I want to be.

A week or so after I was hired, I wrote a joke that alluded to menstruation on a list of "Top Ten Reasons Why This Woman Lost Her Cool." We submitted multiple top ten jokes throughout the day, so I didn't think much of it when I typed, *It was just that time of the month* on the top ten list of reasons some woman went nuts. But when my bosses read it, they called me into their office, cautioned me to delete the joke from my list, and suggested I never submit anything like it again. At first I thought they were just messing with a new writer, but they were not. They said that periods in a joke pitch could be grounds for Dave to fire me.

This helpful talk with my bosses kicked off a new pet project of mine: I assembled an ever-expanding series of Post-its stuck on my desk for the remainder of my time at the *Late Show*, reminders of all the topics that might get me fired if they appeared on a pitch.

The word "abortion" wasn't ever on my list because I didn't need any reminders about that one. The only person in history to get an abortion joke on *Letterman* was Bill Hicks in 1993, during a taping of his twelfth stand-up appearance on the show.

---

*Dave called dick "deal." When writing packets, it always helps to know the host's vernacular.

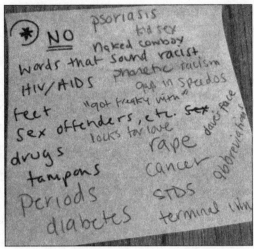

Jena Friedman

You know what really annoys me? These pro-life people. You ever look at their faces? "I'm pro-life!" But they don't look it. [Hicks scrunches his face and crosses his eyes] They just exude the joie de vivre, you know. . . .

"I'm pro-life!" You know, if you're really pro-life, do me a favor, don't lock arms and block med clinics, okay? If you're so pro-life, do me a favor, lock arms and block cemeteries, okay?

The whole set was hilarious and radical, and it still holds up today, but it never even made it to air. Bill's material was apparently too political for the show, and the producers cut it from the final broadcast. The segment aired once, over a decade later in 2009, and only because Dave felt bad that he had censored what, unbeknownst to him, would be Bill Hicks's final *Late Night* performance.* When I learned that it took one of the most inge-

---

* Bill Hicks died of cancer four months after taping that set.

nious comics of his generation sixteen years after his death to get an abortion joke on *Late Night*, I knew mine would never stand a chance. But maybe I'd have better luck at my next gig.

In 2012 I took a job writing and directing field segments for *The Daily Show with Jon Stewart*. Around that time, the Republican war against women was raging yet again. Obama was still president, yes, but decades of conservative efforts to chip away at *Roe v. Wade* were starting to pay off. The brightest minds in the GOP all coalesced around this freshly resuscitated wedge issue and drafted some of the most evilly creative legislation one could ever conceive of (sorry for the pun), like a tax break for fetuses in Michigan, or a bill requiring burials for miscarriages in Indiana. These were all just thinly veiled attempts to force a hearing at the Supreme Court, enshrine fetal personhood into the Constitution, and outlaw abortion nationwide.

For the next three years, almost every other week, a crazy new antichoice bill was being turned into law. I tried to come up with any comedic angle I could think of to convince my bosses at *The Daily Show* to let me cover the issue in a field piece.

Even when I was traveling the country, working on other segments, I would bump up against antichoice protesters. On one shoot, my crew and I stopped by a Planned Parenthood office in Asheville, North Carolina, to get an exterior shot of the facility for a joke about voter suppression ("If we want to level the playing field, move voting booths to places Republicans never go: Planned Parenthoods."*). When I approached the clinic to ask permission to film there, a nervous clinician informed me that the bomb

---

*Many Republicans wouldn't be caught dead in a Planned Parenthood. They get their abortions at private clinics.

squad was en route to investigate a suspicious package—possibly an explosive—tossed onto the clinic's steps.

"You can totally get the shot," she added. "We're all fans of the show and we recognized Aasif [Mandvi] outside. We just wanted to give you a heads up."

"Cool."

I maintained "calm and collected producer" mode, but I was terrified. I had never been so close to a "suspicious package" before (all jokes aside), and it was horribly unnerving. I thanked her, quickly backed out of the building, and turned to see Aasif already in position for the shoot. The suspicious package on the steps didn't *look* like a bomb, but what did I know? My only reference was from movies.

I directed my crew to step away from the "white baggie thing," trying not to arouse suspicion. But then, the moment I yelled, "Action!" our poor camera operator stepped right on top of it. Luckily for him, and for all the rest of us, the bomb didn't go off on impact. A little less lucky for him, said "bomb" was a pile of dog shit hidden under a white plastic bag.

The segment ended up being one of the most viewed *Daily Show* field pieces of all time—partially because it starred the civil rights icon John Lewis, and also because the Republican activist who agreed to be in the segment got fired from his position, as a GOP precinct chair, for his racist remarks (which we captured on camera). My bosses were thrilled, and it gave me renewed faith in the power of comedy to expose injustice.

Now, if only I could turn a comedic lens on the GOP war on women's reproductive rights. With the street cred I'd accumulated from the Asheville segment, I pushed to get a piece about abortion on air. Nonetheless, pitch after pitch went ignored.

THE NEWS STORY [JUNE 2014]: Supreme Court hearings are underway to determine if a 2007 Massachusetts law requiring thirty-five-foot protest-free "buffer zones" outside the state's abortion clinics violates free speech. The buffer zone was enacted for the safety of abortion patients, but protesters claim it's infringing on their First Amendment rights of free speech.

THE COMEDIC PITCH: If the Supreme Court upholds the buffer zones, are antiabortion protesters prepared? Will they be able to reach their audience from thirty-five feet away? Our correspondent sits down with an antiabortion group to find out. They tell us how important proximity is in their ability to protest effectively and that this Supreme Court ruling would violate their First Amendment rights. We're all for free speech, so we decide to help them. In the vein of Waiting for Guffman, *we enlist the expertise of one of New York's most renowned acting coaches to show us the ropes when it comes to "effectively" reaching your audience from a thirty-five-foot distance. After he teaches the protesters the art of projecting, guides them through body movement techniques, and gives them pointers on set design (to make those fetus posters really pop), our protesters stage a "recital" on what they've just learned. Let's call it* Abortion: The Musical, *which we preview in an off-off-Broadway theater. After the show, we ask our test audience of real-life theater patrons if the performance made them not want to get an abortion. Possibly, but it's a moot point, since the only people who go to see theater are over eighty.*

Who wouldn't want to see *Abortion: The Musical*?! Apparently my bosses, who aborted that segment before it even had legs. But I kept them coming.

THE NEWS STORY [MARCH 2014]: The US Supreme Court decided not to block Texas's new abortion law, which activists said had the effect of shutting down about a third of the abortion clinics in the state, leaving twenty-four counties in the Rio Grande Valley without clinics. Part of the new state law requires doctors who perform the procedures to have admitting privileges at a hospital within thirty miles of their clinics. Women's groups and doctors had challenged the law, and a federal court in Texas last month blocked enforcement of that provision the night before it was to take effect. The judge said the law had no medical purpose. But just three days later, on October 31, the Fifth Circuit Court of Appeals overturned that decision, allowing the law to take effect. It said the law was an additional check on a doctor's qualifications.

THE COMEDIC PITCH: Texas's new law is a victory for the pro-life movement, but it's leaving many vulnerable victims in its wake: namely, unwanted buildings. As a result of the Supreme Court ruling, one-third of the state's women's health clinics will be forced to close—and what's going to happen to these abandoned buildings? We sit down with a Texas legislator to congratulate him on this unprecedented legal victory and hear his future real-estate development plans for the state's now closed clinics. When he tells us he hadn't thought about it, we wonder how someone could pass a law without thinking

*about the unintended consequences. We talk to a Texas real-
estate agent, who tells us that buildings left unattended could
become a drain on society and taxpayers . . . they could turn
into crack houses, or worse, shitty fast-food restaurants!
Obviously, a lot of unattended buildings have bright futures,
but mostly in neighborhoods where there's a strong real-estate
market to support them. We return to our lawmaker with this
information. He tells us that people could always adopt these
buildings . . . hmm, are Texans willing to adopt all the unwanted
buildings that this law will create? We hit the streets to find
out. We talk to Texans. Would any of them be willing to adopt
a fourteen-year-old at-risk building? It only costs $10,000/
month . . . does it matter if it's not white? When we don't have
much luck finding a willing tenant, we talk to a spokesperson
for Planned Parenthood, who explains that the law is going to
an appeals court in January . . . so there's still hope for these
buildings!? Not really. She says the Supreme Court ruling was
a nail in the coffin for abortion rights—WHOA, hold up, who
said anything about abortion?*

At one point, a colleague typed my name and the word "abortion" into our *Daily Show* email server and pulled up over thirty
different pitches, none of which ever ended up on air.

Nevertheless, she persisted.

It became a running joke in the field department: When would
Jena ever be able to actualize her fucked-up dream of getting a
story about this taboo topic onto the show?

But then it happened. And all it took was the most insane piece
of legislation ever written.

In July 2014 the state of Alabama signed HB 494 into law. HB

494 grants state funds to lawyers to defend fetuses—against the pregnant teens seeking to abort those same fetuses—in the court of law.

If you're curious about what exactly a "fetus lawyer" is, you're not alone. I had a lot of questions myself. But first, some background: House Bill 494 was a reaction to an existing law in the state of Alabama at the time, whereby if a minor wanted to get an abortion but didn't have parental consent, if maybe her parents didn't approve (or perhaps she couldn't ask her parents for help because her father was the person who impregnated her), the minor could then go to a judge and ask for something called "judicial bypass," whereby the judge would review her case and determine whether the minor was mature enough to get an abortion (as opposed to immature enough to have a child? I don't get it, either).

Under HB 494, the fetus lawyer is legally authorized to operate like any defense attorney (or would they be the prosecutor, in this case?). They can call anyone they wish to the stand, such as the minor's pastor, her basketball coach, her boyfriend, or even the boyfriend's parents, to testify against the minor and on the fetus's behalf. Even if the judge STILL sides with the minor, the fetus lawyer has time on their side. They can always appeal and run out the clock, thereby forcing the minor to carry the pregnancy to full term.

I knew in my bones that this horrific story had all the makings of a great *Daily Show* segment, and this time my bosses agreed. I got the green light, but with one caveat: I needed to find an actual fetus lawyer willing to go on camera.

I often get asked the question, "How do you get people to say such dumb things on camera?" From the outside it sounds like a tall order to get people to participate in comedic videos obviously set up in the hopes that they will say a stupid thing on TV, but the answer is simple: *They don't think what they are saying is dumb.*

With the exception of politicians and cable news pundits, most people are earnest in their convictions and unafraid to espouse them on camera. Furthermore, everyone is a hero in their own story, and everyone wants to be heard.

Those fundamental characteristics of human nature, when combined with a savvy producer and an even better editor (the editor does all the heavy lifting) are often all you need for a solid comedic interview. My colleagues in the field department at the time, all men and very supportive for the most part, did not think that I would be able to find any "fetus lawyer" willing to appear on camera. However, I had something going for me that they did not, something that I think often gets overlooked or underestimated in the world of comedic field production: my gender.

Many people (i.e., men) assume women won't mess with them or make them look stupid on camera (how could we? We're all so unfunny). As a result of this aching blind spot in 49.2 percent of the population, I've personally been able to wrangle all sorts of interesting characters into participating in humorous, self-defeating, and ultimately embarrassing interviews (but more on that later). There also was the very nature of *this* job itself. I assumed that any lawyer out there who lacked the judgment to know it's not okay to put a pregnant minor on trial and interrogate her about her fetus was a lawyer who'd lack the judgment to stay out of my piece. I was right.

Enter Julian McPhillips.

Without hesitation, McPhillips agreed to be in our segment. I roped in Jessica Williams to be my intrepid correspondent and booked our trip to Alabama that afternoon. When I learned that the Alabama chapter of the American Civil Liberties Union—whom we were also interviewing for the piece—was in such fear of being attacked that they couldn't even list their address in the Yellow Pages or post an ACLU banner on their office exterior, I upped our production's safety measures. I moved the hotel we were staying at the night before the shoot to a different city and made sure that we were able to fly back to New York the minute we finished rolling* to avoid any potential post-shoot confrontation. This short turnaround also meant we were going to have to figure out how to put our mark (I promise we didn't call him that) at ease as soon as possible and get all our jokes—I mean *questions*—out quickly.

When we arrived, McPhillips was adamant about giving Jessica a tour of his office in advance of the interview. He wanted her to see all the positive press and accolades he had earned throughout his storied career of rescuing fetuses from abortion. While his enthusiasm was infinite, our time was not. And I didn't think it would benefit our segment to let this guy try to psych Jessica out before the interview. I let Jessica know she should feel free to create distance between herself and the fetus lawyer until roll time, and offered myself as a sacrifice for his attempts to brag about bullying pregnant teen girls. She took her interview prep outside to the car we'd rented, while McPhillips "wowed" me with the tour inside.

When the interview finally started an hour later, McPhillips was at ease and unguarded, and Jessica was incredible.

---

* "I'm so sorry, but we have a flight to catch" is a surprisingly effective way to blow someone off.

JW: You get a call from a fetus seeking legal representation.
Then what happens?

JM: I cannot get a call from a fetus for anything, much less
legal representation.

JW: So how do you meet in confidentiality with your client?

JM: Of course if you've got an unborn child in someone else's
womb, I cannot communicate with them directly. You
know better than to ask that question!

JW: Well, I don't know. You have a crazy-ass job, sir. I don't
know what's in the realm of possibility and what's in the
realm of not possible!

As the segment went on, the questions lobbed at Fetus Lawyer,
Esq. grew in their comedic and investigative power—absurd on
their face, but no more absurd than the premises we'd arrived to
skewer. They were questions like "How do you know that a fetus
is innocent?" and "What about a fetus who eats his own twin in
utero?" As McPhillips continued to earnestly answer questions
pinpointed to undermine the work to which he'd dedicated his life,
he grew increasingly flustered. I watched in awe on the sidelines
and quietly practiced breathing exercises to ensure that I wouldn't
spontaneously laugh and ruin the take. At one point, when Jessica
asked, "Is a zygote a client?" McPhillips looked dumbfounded.
He had no idea what a zygote was (it's a fertilized egg, and if you
didn't know that, either—assuming you're not a fetus lawyer—
you're off the hook).

We ended the segment with a joke that called out Alabama's
underfunded public defender system for diverting funds to fetus
lawyers and away from actual living people in Alabama jails who
needed public defenders. Beyond the bit, if we could just make our

fetus lawyer care about real people in the same way he cared about not-yet-real people, maybe McPhillips could fight for their rights to legal representation as well.

The piece turned out great, but it didn't get McPhillips disbarred or move the needle in any tangible way to improve reproductive rights in the state of Alabama. Not that I thought a comedic field piece would sway hearts and minds in this antichoice state, which coincidentally* has one of the highest rates of infant mortality in the US.

• • •

Just a few years later, in 2017, I left the comfort and security of my behind-the-scenes field producer gig to begin development on a project all my own. After four years of pitching segments that were too dark for network TV, and then too dark for cable TV, I landed on what would later become *Soft Focus with Jena Friedman*. I was collaborating with Adult Swim, an experimental comedy channel, where I was able to double down on the best of my worst impulses. We shot a bunch of sketches and live-action pranks that ended up on the cutting-room floor, including one starring a very real and very unwitting Geraldo Rivera in a fake commercial for a job placement program for rehabilitated repeat sex offenders. He never did realize that we were punking him.

Two of the other segments we shot were what could best be described as live-action, abortion-joke fever dreams. The first segment was a visual joke inspired by the adult baby fetish phenome-

---

* It's no coincidence. According a June 2020 paper in the *International Journal of Environmental Research and Public Health*, US states with more restrictive abortion laws also have higher rates of infant mortality.

non, which hit its peak in 2017 when it made it to a widely shared article on the *Huffington Post*. I thought it would be funny to troll abortion protesters with adult babies protesting at an antiabortion rally as if their own safety was being threatened. Our props department dressed up three amazing male comedian-actors as adult baby protesters and sent them into the field to troll actual antichoice protesters outside an abortion clinic in Queens. Naturally, it created quite a stir, both among the antichoice protesters outside and the overworked, exhausted pro-choice volunteer escorts clearing the way for women seeking care.

In our efforts to be as sensitive as possible (while still making a comedy show), we'd arranged for our actors to embed themselves with the antichoice protesters around the corner from the clinic, out of view and out of the pathway of actual patients. It was edgy, but the scene was only meant to point out the absurdity of the antichoice movement. Plus, politics aside, the sight of three grown-ass men, dressed in adult diapers and marching around with signs that read ADULT BABIES 4 LIFE and AT 2,000 WEEKS HE HAS A HEARTBEAT is undeniably funny. It also confused the shit out of the antichoice protesters and provided some much-needed comic relief to an all-too-tense atmosphere.

Unfortunately (unsurprisingly?), the prank wasn't met with universal acclaim. When clinic escorts got wind that our adult babies were part of a sketch for Adult Swim (a network that didn't always have the best track record with feminist content), they were furious. They posted their photos online and took to Twitter to express their fury. I was alerted to the issue by one of my actors, who is also a friend and brilliant comedian who let me know prochoice activists had identified and started to bully him online. I contacted the activist group immediately to take responsibility, and I tried to explain the progressive intentions of the piece. You might have heard this before, but . . . when you find yourself explaining a joke to someone after the fact, something has gone very wrong.

I fully understood why filming a comedy bit in front of an active abortion clinic might have been a tad insensitive (even though we got the clinic's permission in advance and stayed far away from patients) and apologized to the disgruntled clinic volunteers. We wrapped early, but not before one last prank we wanted to shoot that day while the crew was still on the clock. I'd said I was sorry, but I didn't say we were going to stop filming (don't judge).

For the second prank, I enlisted an acquaintance from New York's downtown comedy scene. I won't name her here to protect her identity, but at the time she had gained a reputation as an activist for openly breastfeeding her son around town, which was cool and radical except for the fact that he was now FOUR YEARS OLD. The most articulate four-year-old I had ever met, yes, but four nonetheless. The pitch, which only a network as insane as Adult Swim would let me actualize, involved my friend, with her breastfed son in tow (or more accurately, on teat), walking up to antiabortion activists as they were protesting to ask them if they would babysit her son while she ran errands.

Breastfeeding is normal and natural, and it's hilarious anytime you can throw that in people's faces (and by that I mean not only the antichoice protesters but also the stoned college kids who watched Adult Swim for cartoons and accidentally stumbled upon my feminist prank show). Furthermore, antiabortion protesters so hell-bent on forcing the rest of us to have kids should at least offer childcare services in exchange. I thought it would be a funny segment to see what would happen if we asked them to do just that; the shock of a woman breastfeeding a kid who was old enough to read was icing on the comedy cake.

What I did not anticipate: the mere sight of a woman breast-feeding was such an anomaly among the antichoice crowd, and such an offense to their senses, that they all instantaneously scattered. We didn't even have time to film any dialogue, because none of the protesters would go near my aggressively breastfeeding friend. The live interaction was amazing, but the footage, which we shot from a distance so as not to blow our cover, was unusable. A Pyrrhic victory. Next time, we'll use hidden cameras.

Afterward, the clinic workers approached our crew (led by our incredible director and my now dear friend, Anu Valia) and thanked everyone. They told us it had been the most effective dispersal of the antichoice harassment teams that encircled their office that they'd ever seen. So pro-choice activists, take note: if you want to get antiabortion trolls off your back, just start breast-feeding in front of them.

The piece never aired, but it felt like a breakthrough. I learned that even if I couldn't get abortion jokes on TV, getting them out there in any way that I could still made an impact.

America's antichoice movement kept gaining steam, emboldened by Donald Trump and his taste for regressive, antiabortion policy and judicial appointees. By 2017, abortion comedy was unfortunately meeting its moment. I would never have imagined I'd one day be speaking on behalf of reproductive justice on the steps of the Supreme Court, but suddenly there I was.

But first a little backstory: If you're unfamiliar with crisis pregnancy centers (aka fake abortion clinics) they're places that pose as legitimate medical establishments to lure in vulnerable pregnant people and then shower them with misinformation. At a CPC you might, for example, "learn" that abortion causes cancer (it doesn't). They're also famous for enlisting unlicensed faux physicians to administer ultrasounds to pregnant people, a practice that is somehow entirely legal in the US.

In 2015 California passed the Reproductive FACT Act, an effort to stop these deceptive CPCs by requiring clinics to post accurate information about where people in the state could seek out real family planning services, including abortions. Immediately, antichoice groups challenged the act, claiming it violated their First Amendment rights—to lie to vulnerable pregnant people. The legal shenanigans worked. By 2018, there were more CPCs operating in the US than real abortion clinics.

When that antichoice challenge, *National Institute of Family and Life Advocates v. Becerra*, finally reached the Supreme Court, Lizz Winstead (the patron saint of abortion comedy, and coincidentally the co-creator of *The Daily Show*) invited me to a National Abortion Rights Action League–sponsored rally in March 2018 to speak alongside other comedians and activists on the Supreme Court steps during oral arguments. Needless to say, I hopped on the next flight out and spent the plane ride from Los Angeles scribbling my speech on a pile of seltzer-soaked napkins (it was a turbulent ride).

The NARAL organizers sent me some talking points, with encouragement to "be funny." My comedy was made for this, but since it was a protest and not a stand-up show, I didn't want to cross the line like I have done so many times before (in comedy, sometimes you have to cross the line to know where the line is). I also didn't want to give right-wing media outlets covering the rally any helpful sound bites to further vilify pro-choice activists (as I had done on election night 2016 when I, freshly stunned by Trump's "win" during Stephen Colbert's *Election Night Special*, boldly exclaimed, "Get your abortions now!" on live TV). So I erred on the side of caution and prepared a somewhat dry, lightly humorous speech.

I didn't anticipate that the antichoice side would be there, too, when I arrived at the Supreme Court's steps the next morning. It was like dueling not-yet-a-baby pianos, with protesters and counterprotesters struggling to scream over each other. It was also cold and rainy. How was I going to get anyone to pay attention in that context? I knew I needed a strong opener to captivate the crowd. But what? And then it hit me. What do you do when you need to get the attention of a distracted, perhaps uninterested audience? I would take a page from the antichoice movement's playbook.

At the last minute, I asked Lizz to change my introduction. When she got up onstage, Lizz grabbed the microphone and enthusiastically introduced me: "We have a superspecial guest that I am so excited to introduce to you. They don't even need credits . . ." The crowd got quiet. Lizz continued, "Ellen DeGeneres!"

The starstruck whispers became a cacophony.

On the side of the stage, I laughed. Nothing brings more joy to a comedian than when you realize a new joke is working. In this case, the payoff was going to be pretty funny. I hesitated before walking onstage, enough to let a *pregnant* pause (I refuse to turn down a good pun) wash over the crowd. Even the antichoicers quieted down. The very real belief that universally beloved (in 2018) celebrity comedian Ellen DeGeneres was about to make a public appearance brought these ideologically opposed factions together for maybe the first time ever. It was a beautiful thing. The excitement was palpable, and I was about to ruin it. I waited a beat for the anticipation to reach its peak, and then I walked onto the stage and took the microphone.

Hi, it's so great to be here!
As many of you can tell, I am not Ellen.

I was greeted by warm laughter from some of the activists. I think the pro-choice protesters got what I was doing immediately. The antis remained quiet, perhaps dumbstruck. I continued.

If you've never been to a comedy club or seen or heard of Ellen DeGeneres, you might think "Hey, that blond white lady . . . maybe that's Ellen. Sure, she seems less funny than I imagine Ellen to be, and definitely so much younger, but maybe Ellen is just having an off day and a great year."

To those of you who knew right away that I'm not Ellen but were expecting to see her, I'm sorry I got your hopes up. I apologize for misleading you with inaccurate information just because I want you to hear what I have to say. At least I didn't waste your time or your energy or try to probe you with a transvaginal wand, when I don't even have a license to do so . . . because that would just be creepy.

I realize this isn't the best analogy, as I am not a fake clinic and Ellen is not an abortion, but let's all just be thankful that we live in a country where you can't legally pretend to be something that you're not just to get people in the door.

Unless of course you're a fake women's health clinic. It's heartbreaking that in America in 2018 there are places that exist for the sole purpose of deceiving vulnerable women and

girls who are just seeking unbiased guidance and fact-based
medical advice. To me that is the opposite of pro-life.

I am here because I'm pro-life. Even though my personal
belief is that life begins at forty, or so I hear, I also believe all
people even under that age should be treated with compassion
and respect, and that starts with access to transparent, fact-
based medical care.

There's an argument that this case is about free speech.
I support the free speech of those who disagree with me—as
long as they are not posing as health-care practitioners and
intentionally misleading people with false information. I also
support the free speech of actual health-care practitioners,
who in some states are forced to lie about abortion just to serve
politicians' ideological agendas. But this case is not about free
speech; it's about the deceptive and dangerous practices that
are going on right now at fake clinics across America. No other
aspect of American life allows for such deception. Minus the
presidency, which will hopefully soon end in impeachment.
[How naive I was.]

So why should it be legal for fake clinics to pose as
something they are not? That is the question we are asking
today, and I hope the court considers it. Okay, that's all from
me. I'm Amy Schumer. Have a nice day.

The speech was appreciated, at least by half the crowd. The
NARAL folks seemed thankful that I stayed on message and in-
jected any humor into the event at all. I felt grateful and lucky that
I was able to show up and support Lizz and her group of hilarious
comedian activists and speak on behalf of a cause I fundamentally
believe in.

I flew back to L.A. feeling inspired but remembering the enormity of what we were up against, cautioning myself not to get too hopeful. Unfortunately, and perhaps inevitably, the conservative majority Supreme Court ended up siding with the fake abortion clinics, on the grounds that, apparently, free speech extends to intentionally misleading pregnant people.

It would take another two years before I would be able to deploy comedy to mess with fake abortion clinics again. I would love to tell you, in great detail, how I, along with the insanely talented team behind *Borat: Subsequent Moviefilm*, managed to pull off one of the greatest crisis pregnancy center pranks of all time, but I signed a confidentiality agreement and I'm not about to break it.

The toxic political climate of 2019, teetering on violence at all times thanks largely to the Racist Tax Evader in Chief, should have discouraged me from touring. But the 2020 election was just around the corner, and I was determined to shout my abortion jokes in any venue in any swing states that would host me. My new material was some of my edgiest, including a joke that is perhaps the closest thing I've ever written as an adult to an actual dead baby joke.

> *I'm in my mid-thirties, so as you can imagine, a lot of my friends are having* [here I touch my stomach and mime holding a baby, then I let my arms fall as I deliver this groaner of a punch line]—*miscarriages.*
>
> *Kids, miscarriages, it's the same thing after thirty-five. Seriously, one in three pregnancies is a miscarriage after the age of thirty-five. It's just something no one talks about, so no one knows, and when it happens to us, we feel even more alone because we don't know how common it is. But*

Everybody Miscarries—*that's a children's book that hasn't been written yet.*

And while we're not talking about it, Republicans are legislating it. In Indiana, there's a new law (HB 1337) that requires women who miscarry to bury the goop. There's no word for the by-products of conception, so let's just call it Gwyneth Paltrow's website. It's hard for us to talk about this stuff. It's hard for female comics to talk about our periods onstage, let alone one with an elbow—

[This usually gets a big audience groan.]

Okay, you're right, that was the worst joke I've ever written. It was funny for about three weeks—then it died.

[more groans]

But I'm not gonna bury that joke! I'm going to keep telling that creepy little corpse of a joke, making everyone uncomfortable—because if men like Mike Pence and Mitch McConnell, who've probably never seen a vagina (allegedly) are able to pass laws that make so many women and girls in America suffer, I'm gonna make sure we all suffer.

Maybe it was in the delivery,[*] but that miscarriage joke worked every time. It worked in red states, like Missouri, and purple states, like Wisconsin. It crushed in Kilkenny and Dublin, Ireland, where abortion had only recently become legal. To this day, that miscarriage joke is truly the darkest joke I've ever performed, but the fact that it's rooted in honesty and inspired by batshit-crazy legislation (which still exists to this day) has insulated me from too much criticism.

---

[*] I will not stop.

Just before the pandemic hit, in February 2020, I was even able to work that miscarriage chunk (not sorry) into a set I performed for Comedy Central on their digital platform, something I could never have imagined a decade ago. In the early 2000s, you couldn't even say the word "abortion" on late-night TV, but now abortion comedy is everywhere.

When I wrote on season two of *The Conners* (formerly the reboot of *Roseanne* . . . I'll get to that later) on ABC, I pitched an idea where Darlene's daughter, Harris, asks her mom to stop by the pharmacy with her to pick up the morning-after pill. It's a short interaction, and the beauty in it lies in how Darlene responds: she supports her daughter and doesn't make it an issue. When I first pitched the scene, my bosses cautioned me that the network might not approve an "abortion story line" (what else is new?), but when I explained to them (of course, almost all men) that the morning-after pill is not an abortion but rather delays the release of an egg from the ovary (which stops a pregnancy from ever occurring), guess what happened next? They listened! It was a small but significant achievement, and to me, it signaled progress. That said, I wasn't invited back to write on the show the following season.

Comedy is powerful like that. It has the ability to disarm, to sugarcoat ideas and make people swallow them, even if they don't agree. Dead baby jokes gave me a power to distract and deflect, but they also taught me how to write comedy that forces people to confront issues like reproductive rights head-on and shock them into attention. It has taken decades for the culture to catch up to the abortion jokes so many comedians have been telling for ages, and now that we're here, maybe the laws won't be too far behind.

Or maybe, this misguided shred of optimism is my best abortion joke yet.

Too Soon

I first saw Mike DeStefano perform on a late weeknight show, to a virtually empty room, at the Boston Comedy Club in New York in 2007. Instantly, I was a fan. His comedy was dark and brutal, and if an audience didn't laugh at his jokes, he would boo *them* until they did. I don't remember how we became friends; we were so different. He was a recovering heroin addict turned stand-up comic, and I was a sheltered college grad whose mother would cry if she knew I was hanging out with a recovering heroin addict. I was living in Chicago at the time, but my cousin had a couch on 96th and Columbus that I would crash on frequently just to dip my toes into the city's overwhelming, sprawling comedy scene.

Mike and I were booked on a couple of seedy shows together, and he was one of the few guys who was kind to me—genuinely, not in a creepy faux-mentor way—a rarity in the club comedy scene back then. When I went back to Chicago, we stayed in touch. From time to time, I would text him dark jokes I had just come up with, and he would text me back words of encouragement, or better yet, an even darker punch line. I was less than two years into stand-up, still finding my voice, and constantly bombing onstage. Positive reinforcement from comics like Mike kept me going. Mike's philosophy was that no topic was off-limits to a comedian: cancer, rape, pedophilia—you name it, you could joke about it. I tended to joke about things I was afraid of, and one of those things was AIDS. I had a lot of AIDS jokes back then—a lot of comics did. Tragedy + time = hacky AIDS jokes.

I was living in Boystown, a predominantly gay neighborhood in Chicago's North Side, and I would often test jokes out at one open mic at a piano bar by my apartment. The audience, mostly gay men over forty, loved my AIDS jokes (or maybe they were just laughing because disposable incomes and no kids are the secret to happiness). Either way, testing out my new material on that crowd gave me confidence that if the demographic most impacted by something so tragic could appreciate my fucked-up jokes about it, maybe everyone else could, too.

Whenever I would text one of my new AIDS jokes to Mike, each more fucked-up than the previous and none I feel comfortable sharing here, Mike would always text back *ha* or *:-)*. This was an era before emojis. But one day, he texted back something else: *Did you know my wife died of AIDS?*

I didn't think much of it before I responded, *Ha! Good one.* I waited for his response, but he didn't reply. Mike had such a fucked-up sense of humor—he always replied. I waited a few more minutes. The silence was disconcerting. I began to second-guess myself. He was joking, right? Mike's wife didn't *really* die of AIDS . . . as far as I knew, he didn't even have a wife? He was a relatively new friend and we really didn't know each other outside of comedy, but it couldn't be. Right?

A sickening feeling crept over me. What if he was serious? Mike never mentioned being married, but why would he if his wife was dead? I decided to give him a call.

"Hey, you were joking, right?"

He paused before responding, "No—" Part of me thought this was just some extended bit, but I could tell by the tone in his voice that he was being earnest. My heart sank.

"Oh my God, I am so sorry, Mike."

He reassured me: "Your joke is still funny." I couldn't even pretend to laugh. I felt like such an insensitive asshole. I apologized again. "Really, it's okay," he assured me. "I assumed you didn't know, either that or you're just a psychopath." He laughed. "So I figured I should tell you." I replayed in my mind all the many times I had texted him dumb, thoughtless jokes about something that had so intimately affected him. I imagined how awful it must have been for someone who had experienced such a profound loss to be constantly reminded of it by a twenty-four-year-old open-micer whose most tragic event in her life up until that point had been the death of a grandparent she was too young to remember. I still cringe thinking about it. I don't recall the rest of our conversation that day, other than that Mike swore he wasn't offended and somehow made *me* feel okay about it all, as if *I* was the one who needed comfort. I hate to say it, but maybe I did.

After the call, I vowed to be a little more careful with my comedy. I would at least try to make sure that any joke I wrote about a taboo subject wasn't also unnecessarily cruel. I thought my brief friendship with Mike might be over after that, but a few weeks later, he called.

"I need a favor," he said. I was so relieved.

"Anything."

"I just got offered a gig at the Lakeshore Theater and I need your help. . . ." The Lakeshore Theater was the coolest spot for alternative comedy in Chicago (for the few years that it existed before it got bought out and became a Laugh Factory). It was also a place that was incredibly supportive of young comics, and I performed there often. Mike knew that I was friendly with the theater's owner (the Lakeshore's Chris Ritter was one of the only club owners in Chicago who would book me), and since Mike didn't yet have an agent, he asked me to help negotiate his rate. I was honored.

"The offer is eight hundred dollars for one night. Can you tell them I'll do it for a thousand?"

"Sure!"

"It's not about the money, it's about the principle. I can't let people know I'd do a road gig for less than a thousand dollars a night."

"Okay, cool." I didn't know anything about the business, so I just listened intently as he went on. "If you can bump up my rate to a thousand, you can have the other two hundred and open for me."

It was a dream to open for Mike. I would have done it for free. I think I even told him that, but he insisted on paying me. He also gave me shit for offering to open for free.

Part of the reason why the Lakeshore Theater lasted only a few years was precisely because it was cool. The management supported lesser-known comics who they genuinely found funny and not just famous comics who could sell out a room. The management also refused to do what almost all the mainstream comedy clubs were doing at the time: requiring patrons to buy at least two drinks in addition to tickets to offset the venue's overhead costs (also known as "the two-drink minimum"). In fact, the Lakeshore was so damn cool and so adamant about doing things differently that they built a whole marketing campaign around their alternative approach to comedy. I remember the theater's walls were decorated with edgy posters that read things like, THERE'S NOTHING FUNNY ABOUT A TWO-DRINK MINIMUM and DANE COOK SUCKS AND YOU KNOW IT. I personally had nothing against the guy, but I do miss the days when the comedy world was united in a mutual disdain for Dane Cook.

I have so many wonderful memories of performing at the Lakeshore Theater. One time, in 2008, a bunch of young comics and I were performing on a weekend show there when Robin Williams—yes, THAT Robin Williams—stopped by to do a surprise set[*]. He was in town for a TV taping and was working out new material for a special he was planning to shoot soon. I don't know what compelled me, but during a lull in the conversation in the greenroom, I broke the silence by inviting him to perform the following night on a little show I was producing and hosting at a hole-in-the-wall bar in Boystown.

The show was called *Entertaining Julia*, after my friend Julia, the bartender at the Town Hall Pub, a nondescript dive bar where she let me host a weekly show. We always went late and featured an eclectic mix of local comedians and musicians who I had met while performing on other shows and open mics around town. I didn't really think Robin Williams was going to take up my offer, but the next night he did. In fact, he arrived a half hour before the show even started. Word traveled fast, and pretty soon almost every young comic in Chicago was piled into that dingy bar, waiting for

---

[*] Lyons, Margaret, "Robin Williams's Surprise Sets," Chicagoist.com, May 5, 2008.

this living legend to perform. Robin sat through the entire show, too, and waited patiently as he watched all the other comics on the lineup. At about ten p.m., he took the stage. In the greenroom the previous night, Robin seemed more somber and reserved than his onstage persona had led me to believe he'd be. Apparently, he had been going through some issues in his personal life, and you could feel the sadness in his demeanor. But the moment he walked onstage, his energy shifted and he morphed into the manic comic genius that had made him a superstar. In front of a room packed with young, wide-eyed comedy nerds, Robin strayed from the club-friendly material he had been working out the previous night and delivered a jaw-dropping performance that felt honest, spontaneous, and frenetic in the best way. He talked candidly about his divorce, his sobriety, and his fame, among other things, to thunderous cackles from the excited audience of starstruck young comedian fans. It remains to this day one of the funniest performances I have ever seen live.

Mike DeStefano's set at the Lakeshore the night that I opened for him is another memorable performance I'll never forget, and not only because he too was brilliant but also because I bombed harder on that show than I have ever bombed in my entire life.

Prior to the show, I was incredibly nervous. Mike's crowd was not my crowd. They were mostly middle-aged white men, a lot of *Opie and Anthony* fans, some people in recovery, and many others who should have been. Keenly aware of how I imagined this crowd might receive my comedy, I pored over all my material for the weeks leading up to the show to prep my best ten minutes that I thought would go over well with Mike's fans. To my surprise, the set did go quite well and I was so incredibly relieved. That is, until we broke for intermission.

Most comedy club shows don't hold intermissions between acts. They don't need to because they require audiences to purchase at least two drinks during the evening. But because the Lakeshore was "so cool" and didn't force their audience pay for drinks, to make sure that people bought drinks (and more importantly, that the venue actually made money), they would hold an intermission (or sometimes two) right in the middle of a show, just as it was building up energy. Mike didn't know that his show would be interrupted by an intermission, so when he found out as it was happening in real time, he turned to me with a change of plans.

"I'm not going out to a cold room. You're going to have to do a few more minutes to warm them up." I understood what he meant, and I would have totally been down to do more material. The only problem was I DIDN'T HAVE ANY MORE MATERIAL. I had just blown through all my best jokes to make an audience of men I'd be afraid to be alone in a room with laugh. If I went out onstage without any good bits, they'd eat me alive. I started to panic. Mike thought this was hilarious.

"You'll be great. You have the rest of intermission to figure it out." I had only been doing comedy for about a year and a half, and it took me that long write a solid ten minutes of material. How was I going to come up with another five in the span of a fifteen-minute intermission? This was a late-night Saturday show, too, the time slot notorious for attracting the rowdiest and least forgiving crowds. I couldn't just wing it. I had to be funny or I would lose the audience and all hell would break loose. I ordered a drink and jotted down some ideas, none of which gave me any confidence in how this was going to go ("What's the deal with intermissions?" Nope.). When the intermission ended, the audience shuffled back to their seats and I slowly walked onstage. I wasn't even more than a minute into a half-baked new joke when some guys in the second row started to heckle me.

"You're not funny!" one of them yelled in between chugs of the beers he was double fisting. There's really no more damaging heckle a comic can get than "You're not funny," especially when it's true. I was scared and unprepared. I had no more material to fall back on, and I was too nervous to try to improvise. And on top of my lackluster performance, I now had to respond to these drunken guys in the front of the audience. If I pretended not to hear their taunts, it would look as if I wasn't in control of the show, and the rest of the crowd might turn on me as well. I was backed into a corner. I had to say something, but what?

Over the years, I've gotten better at dealing with hecklers. But as a young comic, I often struggled. I remember on one of my first shows, a guy yelled, "Can I get a blow job?" I responded by simply walking offstage. Another time, I was totally thrown by what I thought was a heckler in the front row, who, anytime I asked a rhetorical question, would attempt to answer it in earnest. It turns out he was just a superfan with an autism spectrum disorder who did not understand that my questions were setups to jokes and didn't require actual answers. Thankfully, I was able to see his face and infer pretty quickly that there was something else going on before I responded to him, with appropriate sensitivity and compassion, of course!

There are many schools of thought on how to handle hecklers: one is to have an arsenal of comebacks you've written in advance (Mike had a great line that went something like "It's not my fault you don't have a funny friend to hang out with"). Another is to comment on the heckler's appearance or joke about the size of their genitals (not my thing, it's just what I've seen other comics do). A third way to deal with hecklers is to just say whatever comes to mind, as long as it's not too mean-spirited, and hope for the best (which is what I do now, and it almost always works).

That night I opened for Mike I was still relatively inexperienced in dealing with hecklers, so I went the obvious route and decided to make fun of their looks, which stood out because they happened to be three white dudes dressed like '90s rappers. I started brainstorming various comebacks, but before I could determine how best to shut down three obnoxious drunk white men appropriating Black culture, one of them shouted again, "You're not really funny." I instantly fired back, "You're not really Black."

The audience grew silent. Had I crossed the line? These guys were the problem, not me . . . right? Then it dawned on me that no one else in the 338-seat room saw that the drunken hecklers were white. For all they knew, I was just some unfunny white lady comic making a snide remark about a random heckler's race. The crowd started to turn on me. Even though my targets were very much deserving of ridicule, my words got lost in translation and I wasn't sure how to get the crowd back on my side. The next minute felt like an eternity. I didn't know what else to do, but I did know that the longer I stayed out onstage without material, the worse it would get. When another heckler chimed in, "We want Mike!" I didn't even attempt to do my next joke. I quickly introduced Mike and ran offstage.

I sat alone in the greenroom and stared at my flushed face in the mirror as I struggled to hold back tears. Maybe I wasn't cut out to be a stand-up comic after all? A few moments later, my pity party was interrupted by the sound of thunderous laughter from the crowd. I walked over to the side of the stage to check out what was going on and saw that Mike was killing it. A true pro, he played on the uncomfortable tension my awkward bomb had left behind and utterly slayed.

Mike caught me after the show and laughed it off. He even thanked me for bombing so hard. "Sometimes an audience needs to see that comedy can be hard, for them to really appreciate it," he teased. I deserved it.

That was the last show I got to do with Mike. The following year, he went on to be a finalist in season seven of NBC's *Last Comic Standing*. He was universally beloved by his peers, about to perform a one-man show in New York, and was on the brink of becoming a household name when he died suddenly of a heart attack at the age of forty-four.

Mike wasn't like anyone I had ever met before or anyone I would have met had I not gotten into comedy. He was brutal and profane onstage and yet so kind and empathetic offstage. I'm a better person and a better comedian because of my brief friendship with Mike DeStefano. He's why I always try to make sure that the dark jokes I tell have a larger point and purpose than shock value. And if he were still alive, he would definitely give me shit for saying that.

Cutting My Teeth

My "rock bottom" started out as a pretty ordinary Monday night in New York City. I was about to turn twenty-eight, barely making enough money to get by, and deeply frustrated and self-conscious with where I was in my career. A few weeks earlier, my dad's father had passed away. I didn't really know him when I was a kid. My mom often jokes that it was probably for the best, as he was apparently not very warm or loving. But prior to his death, I got to know him a little bit, as he would call me from time to time to tell me how worried he was about my decision to pursue comedy. He thought I should seriously consider grad school. I thought it was funny that someone who had seemed to exhibit no interest in the first twenty-seven years of my life was now so invested in my future, but I would hear him out on our infrequent calls, mostly because every time I did, he'd follow up by sending a small check in the mail, along with a letter, reprimanding me for cashing it.

The money from my dad's dad (it feels weird to call him Grandpa) wasn't life-changing (maybe a few hundred dollars a few times a year), but I welcomed any help I could get. I was burning the candle at both ends, working shitty Craigslist jobs by day and bartending and performing stand-up at night. I was also submitting writing packets left and right to various late-night shows, determined to get a coveted staff-writing job. Applying for these elusive writing gigs felt like a full-time job itself, and every rejection felt like a critical blow to my confidence and my future aspirations in comedy. Once, after I pulled a few all-nighters busting my ass to submit a last-minute packet to write for Chelsea Handler's *Chelsea Lately*, only to be told they weren't looking for New York comics, I broke down and cried in front of my whole class while doing hip exercises in a Bikram yoga studio. In my defense, apparently a lot of people cry during hot yoga.

This is all just to say that I was already at the end of my rope. I had just finished a five-minute set at the Bowery Poetry Club open mic, which was the highlight of my week and the only consistent thing I had going on to help me mark the passage of time.

When I first moved to New York (Hoboken for a month and then Williamsburg briefly and *then* the East Village) in 2008, the Bowery Poetry Club was one of the coolest experimental performance art venues in all of Manhattan, and the Monday open mics were legendary. The space was cavernous (by New York City standards) yet cozy, with tall exposed-brick walls covered in art for sale, a bar in the back corner, and a large, inviting stage, front and center. My dear friend Jessica Delfino, a "dirty folk rock" comedian, once described the scene at the BPC as "a circus-like church of the bizarre and beautiful, with a cult following of students, stars, and street rats." It was a weird collection of comedy, burlesque, performance art, and anything else cool downtown in the first decade of the century.

Within this carnival of misfits were now-notable comedians and writers like Reggie Watts, Jonathan Ames, Kristen Schaal, and Eric André, as well as pretty much every unknown and alt comic in the city. We would all stop by at some point at least once a month between the hours of seven p.m. and one a.m. to work out four minutes of material to the warm, enthusiastic room. It wasn't just another open mic; it was a community and one of the things that kept me going in my early years in New York. Looking back on it, that time feels so special and like the end of an era, when Manhattan was still an artistic and creative hub, and not just a playpen for billionaires, a time when even the most obscure artists, unsuccessful comedians, and total weirdos could actually live and perform in a city, without taking a bus and three trains to get there.

That particular night I was exhausted and maybe also dehydrated (I had taken a hot yoga class the day before). My set went over well. I told a new joke onstage that kind of bombed, but in a good way, as bombing was encouraged in that crowd because it meant that you were doing something new or outside your comfort zone. That night I had also had a glass of wine on an empty stomach—or was it two glasses?—so I was already feeling a little buzzy when my friend Ben invited me down to the basement to smoke a joint with him and some other comics (one of them was a pretty famous comedian and his wife who I will not name here, but whose celebrity is actually part of the story). I wasn't much of a pot smoker, but I didn't have anywhere to be the next morning, so I headed down to the basement to join them.

As Ben passed around the joint, the famous comedian regaled us with some crazy story that I cannot recall. I tried to mute how starstruck I was with another small hit. Bad move. As the comedian continued with his story, I started to get dizzy.

Something didn't feel right. I wondered if what we were smoking was actually pot. I realized that if ever I was going to smoke bad pot, it was probably going to be with Ben. I took a deep breath as I tried to manage my rising nausea. I began to see black dots in front of me and recalled a story my mom had told me about a time her "friend" had "accidentally" smoked pot laced with an unknown substance and realized something was off when the chair in her kitchen started to move on its own. She said that her friend tried to remain calm and let the chair walk toward her, and a few hours later she was fine. Was I about to see that chair? I felt light-headed, but I had the wherewithal to feign laughter at the right points in whatever story the comedian was telling, even though what he was saying sounded increasingly far away. And then, everything went dark.

I woke up on the ground, with my face flat against the cold concrete floor. I felt a pain radiating out of my chin, and a warm, metallic liquid gushing out of my mouth.

"Somebody call 911!" screamed the comedian. Was he talking about me? I felt so embarrassed, and my first instinct was to calm him down.

"I'm fine," I assured him as I spat what felt like shards of pebbles out of my mouth, only to realize they were my teeth. The comedian's wife knelt down, put her arm around me, and helped me up.

"I think you just fainted," she whispered. "Are you okay?"

I was in a daze.

"Yeah, I'm fine."

"Guys, she's okay. She just fainted," she assured her husband, Ben, and another bystander, whose name I forget, maybe because she was standing right next to me when I fainted and didn't catch me or even try to break my fall. The comedian's wife helped me up.

"Are you okay to stand?" I nodded. I was. "I've fainted from smoking pot before, too. Come with me," she said as she led me to the bathroom. At this point, my hand was covering my mouth to try to stop the blood that was leaking out of it.

In the bathroom, she handed me a ball of wet paper towels to clean off the other blood I didn't even know was staining my face. I looked into the mirror to survey the damage—holy shit. Three front teeth, gone. My first thought, as I stared at what looked like an anti-meth PSA, was, *My mom is going to kill me.*

The comedian's wife, who was also a comedian, writer, and producer in her own right, went into full-on producer mode.

"We need to take care of this now," she said to her husband. To this day, I've never been more comforted by the word "we." I didn't know how to interpret it. I didn't have to. She continued, "Trust me, you're not gonna want to deal with this in the morning. We gotta get you to a dentist . . . now." It was past midnight. I knew you could get almost anything at any hour in New York City, like sushi for breakfast or a pedicure at four a.m., but cosmetic dentistry? Her husband looked shell-shocked—it was actually incredibly jarring to see someone so funny look so dead serious—and I tried to flash him a smile to temper the abject fear in his eyes, but my jack-o'-lantern face only scared him more. His wife took his phone. "You have Chuck's* number, right?" I didn't know who Chuck was, but I assumed he was either their dentist or a celebrity fixer.

The comedian dialed it for her. "Hey, Chuck, we have a little emergency. [Redacted comedian] just fell and broke some teeth and he has to be on TV tomorrow. Can we stop by your office to-

---

* Chuck was not the dentist's real name.

91

night?" The next thing I knew, the comedian, his wife, and I were in a cab en route to an after-hours dental appointment at two a.m. in SoHo. A New York moment if there ever was one.

When the dentist arrived, the comedian's wife told him what really happened and that it was actually I, some random, unknown, and far less successful comic (my words, not hers!) who broke her teeth and needed them fixed. The dentist surprisingly took it in stride. He was clearly a fan of the actually famous comedian and happy to help. I was embarrassed to admit that I had been smoking pot, but then the comedian joked (or at least I think he was joking) that we should all do nitrous, and I suddenly felt less self-conscious.

The dentist spent the next hour patching up the wreckage in my mouth while the comedian and his incredible wife kept us company. The swelling made it hard to assess the damage, so the dentist fashioned a temporary bridge and scheduled me in to see him again in a few days. I didn't have dental insurance, but it didn't matter. Even if I had insurance, this dentist-to-the-stars-who-hadn't-yet-sold-out-and-moved-to-L.A. didn't take it. I tried not to think about the cost, which I imagined would be exorbitant. This was a medical emergency, and I was just thankful this fancy dentist was able to come through at a moment's notice.

For the next few years, I went back to that dentist, who also had his own headshot and once asked me to sneak his artisanal, homemade mouthwash (I kid you not) into the bathrooms at *The Daily Show* offices. On one occasion, after a crown on one of the broken teeth came loose and I went to the dentist to fix it, I asked him how much it was going to cost beforehand because the frequent appointments were bleeding me dry. He assured me, "Don't worry about it." When the appointment ended, his assistant handed me a bill for $2,000! Finally, after so many dental appointments to fix my poor front teeth, I stood my ground.

"'Don't worry about it' doesn't mean you can charge me two thousand dollars without a heads-up." The dentist nodded. He instructed his assistant to come up with an amount that felt fair and left to tend to other clients, I mean patients. His assistant guided me to a back room, out of earshot of everyone in the waiting room, apparently to negotiate. I didn't realize medical care was negotiable, but here we were.

"Fifteen hundred," she offered. I blanched.

"That's not the point. I've been coming to you guys for over two years now, I have spent thousands of dollars to fix my teeth, and I'd like a little transparency."

"One thousand," she said. I looked at her, confused.

"I'm not trying to haggle for my medical care. I just want to be able to trust that when Dr. Smith* says, 'Don't worry about it,' I'm not going to get another bill for two thousand dollars."

"Five hundred."

I thought about it for a moment, kind of shocked by my newly adept bargaining skills.

"Fine," I said, exasperated and somewhat put off by what now felt like a Mafia-run dental shop. I swiped my credit card, left their office, and never returned.

When all was said and done, the total out-of-pocket expenses for my dental work and various ancillary appointments for two crowns and an implant to fix my three broken front teeth over a period of two years cost roughly $12,104.16. I had trauma-bonded with that dentist and he really did come through for me in my

---

* Sorry to any Dr. Smiths out there. This is also a pseudonym.

darkest hour. Did I get taken? Probably, but I also had no other alternative.

Sometimes in life you get lucky, and sometimes you get very unlucky, and sometimes you get both. There's no way I would have been able to pay for all that out-of-pocket cosmetic dentistry had it not been for a little financial windfall I had received a few weeks before in the form of a matured savings bond bequeathed onto me from my dear dad's father. The eeriest part is that my inheritance from him was valued at almost the exact amount it cost to fix my teeth . . . to the tens. Sometimes I wonder if my fainting spell was less the result of smoking pot on an empty stomach than my estranged grandpa's ghost strangling me from beyond the grave as a warning to get a real job.

Thankfully, it didn't work.

Sex Pays

When I was starting out in comedy,* I took on all sorts of odd jobs to pay the rent. One of those jobs was as a sex columnist for a men's fitness magazine. What qualified me for the job? Absolutely nothing. Why did I do it? Because it paid!

This was my first experience attempting to inform and lightly troll men at the same time, and it was actually pretty fun. If you're a man and you bought this book because you stumbled upon my Adult Swim show in between reruns of *Rick and Morty*, this chapter is for you!

Q: I've been seeing the same girl on the bus each morning, and we make eye contact, and once we actually smiled at each other, but that's as far as it's gone. I've even started staying on her bus, the local, and not switching

---

* Okay, fine, I was eight years in, but I had just left *The Daily Show* and money was tight!

to the express, so I'll run into her. I want to talk to her, but how should I go about it? I don't want to come off like a stalker.

A: Are you a stalker? If so I'd say just keep doing what you're doing. If not, please continue reading. For the non-stalker who plots his work route to coincide with his crush's commute but wants to take it to the next level, I'd say the next best move after smiling at her on a daily basis is to just break the ice with a simple greeting like "hi." If she says "hi" back, that's a good sign. Also, pay attention to her body language. If she opens up and turns toward you, maybe continue with a provocative follow-up like "Hi, my name's _____." If she responds by telling you her name, maybe proceed with a more nuanced question, like asking her where she works. If she tells you Planned Parenthood, tell her that you applaud her heroic efforts in such a scary, hyper-politicized environment to provide communities with affordable and quality health care, such as mammograms, contraceptives, and STD screenings, and ask if there's anything you can do to help. She'll tell you that you can donate to Planned Parenthood via their website at plannedparenthood.org. Your next best bet is to get out your phone and make a really generous donation. After all, it's the least you can do! Once your phone is out, slyly ask your crush for her number. Twenty dollars says she'll give it to you, and so will I, you stud.

Q: What are the sexiest things I can say to a woman during sex to really turn her on?

A: In terms of pillow talk, context is key. For example, is this woman a one-night stand or a burgeoning relationship? Is she your girlfriend who you're trying to spice things up with or an ex who you hate? My advice for the woman you don't really know but want to see again is to err on the side of caution. Steer away from anything too vulgar, unless she initiates it. Nothing is less sexy than hearing the word "shlong" out of a guy's mouth. It tips us off to the fact that you watch too much porn. If you feel compelled to speak during sex, maybe start off with something like "you're beautiful." Ugh, I just got cheese chills writing that, but unfortunately, it is something a lot of women like to hear. If you're feeling ballsy, you could add "even more beautiful than my ex—who died in a fire." Is that too dark? It'll totally get her going, especially if it's true! Women are suckers for ghost stories, particularly in bed.

As for the girlfriend you're trying to spice things up with, if she's cool and doesn't have a heart condition, you might want to try scaring her. You can have a lot of fun with a woman who's not a gun owner. Like on a night when she thinks she's home alone, maybe don a ski mask and sneak up from behind.* Once you pin her to the ground, gently place your gloved hand over her mouth and whisper, "Shh." She'll start to cry, and that's when you pull off the mask and surprise her with your adorable, recognizable face. Her cortisol levels will be so high she'll be putty in your hands.

---

* I'm pretty sure this whole bit got cut.

Q: A friend of mine says his girlfriend gives him a blow job every morning so he'll stay happy and not feel tempted to cheat. I think that's a GREAT idea—how should I bring it up with my girlfriend?

A: However you want, but definitely start with an apology. Healthy, mutually satisfying relationships shouldn't involve coercion or manipulation. Not to knock blow jobs (for the record, I'm not sex-negative, just negative), but your friend sounds like he's the one who sucks (pun intended, they don't pay me a paltry stipend for nothing!). Maybe I woke up on the wrong side of the bed, but at least it wasn't next to some lame dude who would try to manipulate me into blowing him on a daily basis. Jesus Christ.

Q: A girl I've texted, who seems interested, has now canceled dates twice, once saying she had to work late and once saying she had to go home for the weekend because her dad was sick. Should I keep pursuing her or let it die? If I do, what should I say? I don't want to come across as desperate.

A: Aw, buddy, it sounds like she's not interested. But she could also have a demanding job or better yet, a sick dad, so all hope is not lost! Let's say, on the bright side, that her dad is SUPER sick. I would suggest giving her a call. When she doesn't pick up (because she's either in the hospital with her dying dad or because she's just not that into you), leave a voice message telling her you hope everything is okay and that you would love to see her again (after her dad gets better or dies). Maybe don't mention her dad in the voice mail, but do reach out. I know this response sounds like I'm teasing you, and I am, but mostly because I think there's too much hesitancy on all our parts as far as text etiquette. In all honesty, when you really do like someone, you have nothing to lose by calling or sending a text or even an email. Worst-case scenario, it will show her that you care and yes, it may read as slightly desperate, but you ARE desperate—I mean, you're asking me for advice. So just own it! Send her one more short text that tells her how you feel and leave it at that. If she doesn't respond, you'll know she's not feeling it, perhaps because she's working through the devastating loss of the man closest to her or because she's just not attracted to the type of guy who would stress out over a text message, and you'll be able to move on.

Q: My ex just sent me a friend request on Facebook. Should I accept?

A: Your ex JUST sent you the request? She must have recently gotten divorced and is now prowling social media, looking to have as much sex as possible with old flames so as not to increase her number of sex partners. It's actually still a thing some women care about (because we live in a culture that shames women for being human). But that's beside the point. The real question is, why are you still on Facebook?

Q: My girlfriend is good friends with one of her old boyfriends and sees him occasionally for dinner. She

swears there's nothing romantic between them and that they're just great pals. Should I be worried?

A: Should you be worried? Yes, always, about everything . . . except for this. From Al Qaeda to zoonotic diseases, there are plenty of things to keep you up at night, but whether or not your girlfriend still has feelings for her ex isn't one of them. Why? Because even if she did, there's nothing you can do about it. Not. A. Thing. (I get paid per word.) Look, maybe she is plotting to get back together with him. If that's the case, it's not like you'd be able to stop them. But that's not what's going on—she probably enjoys getting dinner with him because she never was in love with him to begin with and likes that he always pays . . . I'm writing from experience. Be careful not to over-involve yourself in this, as anything you do to limit the amount of time she spends with him will come across as controlling and insecure. She clearly likes you, and there's a reason she's not still dating her old boyfriend. Maybe it's because he wouldn't let her stay friends with her exes?

Q: I used to be pretty lucky with women, but lately I've been striking out right and left—one date, and that's it, they're done. How can I figure out what I'm doing wrong?

A: Hmm, sounds like you may have lost your mojo. It could just be a seasonal funk, or maybe there's something going on with you beneath the surface that you're not acknowledging (maybe something in your life has shaken your confidence, like a job loss or increased awareness of your own mediocrity?). I don't know. I'm not a therapist. But I do know that what happens once you lose your mojo is that you start fixating on it, which only makes things worse. Mojo-less you becomes needy and insecure, you start smelling like desperation, your friends start blowing you off because you're too much of a bummer to be around, and then the next thing you know, you're writing to sex columns in fitness magazines, searching for answers . . . not to worry! I've got your back. My first thought: What about dating a different type of woman (an equally desperate one?) or meeting women in places you wouldn't normally pick them up (a retirement home or an AA meeting?)? That might help you get out of your funk. Or if that doesn't work, maybe try picking up men? They'll fuck anything.

Q: I had sex with the stripper at a bachelor party the other night. That's not so bad, right? Unfortunately, it was *my* bachelor party. I feel terribly guilty about it, and I know I'll never do it again (I was pretty drunk). But I'm getting married in a few days—should I tell my fiance? I don't know which would be worse—her finding out now that I did it, or finding out later that I wasn't honest.

A: Oh jeez. Did you at least wear a condom? You know, it doesn't matter, the scenario sucks all around. If I were your friend, I would probably advise you not to tell her, because she's not going to be happy about it. I mean,

I'm guessing, but what do I know? Maybe you sleeping with sex workers right before your wedding is her secret fetish? You should find out. But if you think she'll be pissed, the next question to ask yourself is how fun do you want your wedding to be? If you want a fun wedding, shut the fuck up and be the best groom you can be and never do something like that again. However, if you are seriously committed to building a lasting foundation of a strong, honest marriage, then come clean and tell her. Worst-case scenario, she calls off the wedding, you develop herpes and/or something worse (HIV is actually the new diabetes, so I'm thinking more along the lines of Ebola, which is weirdly sexually transmitted, too), the stripper you slept with ends up pregnant with a Zika baby (I should probably cut this) and then leaves you with it, forcing you to raise the child on your own, which is even harder now that President Cruz has gotten rid of pretty much all of our country's social safety nets. You're forced to quit your job so that you can have more flexible work hours to care for Iggy (I decided to name your son Iggy, hope that's okay) but are still finding it hard to make ends meet. One day you call your ex and tell her you miss her and that you want nothing more in the world than to be with her. She says that she appreciates the call, and even calls you "sweet" (which is actually the worst thing to call someone, because it means you no longer occupy space in their heart and they don't even care enough about you to be bitter). Then she tells you that she's over you and has moved on. You're devastated at first, but then you look at little baby Iggy, who's smiling up at you, and you realize that your love for him is stronger than any love you have ever felt before and that he has made your life whole in a way no other relationship ever could and things happen for a reason and finally you feel at peace.

Q: My girlfriend is fantastic in bed, and I really enjoy being with her. She's a great person, but on a romantic level, I can't actually see myself ever marrying her. Should I break it off?

A: What constitutes a "romantic" level? She's great in bed, you enjoy being with her, AND she's a great person . . . but what, she doesn't cough up rose petals when she cums? Maybe she's too busy being great in and out of bed to put effort into lame, socially constructed gestures that constitute romance. If that's a deal breaker, then yeah, you should probably break it off—for her sake, Mr. Romantic.

Q: My girlfriend said she was okay with me watching porn, but the other night she said she wasn't into getting together, so I went online. . . . Well, the next day she asked if I'd jerked off to it and got upset when I said yes (hey, I didn't want to lie). So, is getting off to porn really okay, or are women just lying when they say that?

A: Every woman is different. But also, of course it's okay. Personally, I'm fine with my fictional boyfriend watching porn, as long as it's not illegal or on my computer. I don't know the details of your relationship, but from what you described in the two sentences above that the copy editor probably paraphrased, it sounds like your situation is less about your interest in jerking off to porn and more about your need for your girlfriend's approval on matters she's not really supposed to weigh in on. At the end of the day, it's your body, your choice.

Q: Are girls into flavored condoms? Is that something I should try?

A: No. Nothing is worse than a vaguely familiar flavor of something with hints of latex and dick.

Q: I don't want to sound naive, but sometimes when a girl performs oral on me, she sounds like she's gagging, and her eyes start watering. . . . Is that just part of the whole thing, or am I doing something wrong?

A: If someone is gagging and crying while they're going down on you, maybe it just wasn't in the cards. Perhaps you guys should just be friends? I don't know your life, but from my personal experience, oral sex doesn't involve dry heaving and tears. If you do like the person, you can always ask her if she's comfortable. If you can't make out what she's saying because your dick is in her mouth, take it out and ask again.

Q: My girlfriend asked me how many women I've had sex with—should I be honest? It's not, like, an army, but it's more than a handful. . . . And what if she tells me

she's been with the whole football team? I'm not sure I'm ready for that.

A: No. Never be honest. Tell her you can't remember the number because until her, no one has counted.

Q: Man, do I love morning sex. Her, not so much. She says she's not awake yet, she's worried about the day at her job, she doesn't feel "pretty" yet. Sometimes she'll do it, though, but it's kind of a "mercy fuck." Is there anything I can do to get her more into it?

A: Uh, you lost me at "she says she's not awake yet." Rule of thumb, never coerce women into any sexual activity. That's literally why I agreed to write this column—to hammer that point home. Now assuming that she is awake and consenting but just "not in the mood," maybe you could work a little harder to get her in the mood. Start by doing whatever constitutes foreplay during non-morning sex (whisper sweet nothings in her ear, softly touch the nape of her neck, pick her up from the airport). . . . If that doesn't work, you can always become nocturnal, sync your waking up to whenever she's in the mood, and then you can have all the morning sex you want, but just make sure she's up for it—literally and figuratively. Otherwise it's not morning sex, it's assault.

Q: She likes to have sex during "that time of the month," but I'm not into it. What should I do?

A: You should get into it! Period sex is an age-old ritual that solidifies the bond between a woman and her prey, I mean sex partner. I'm not a doctor, but I hear it also increases relationship satisfaction, longevity, and penis size. And if that's not compelling enough, it's a great way to create a crime scene in case you ever need to fake your own murder-suicide.

Q: I'd really like to try a threesome with two women—I hear it's incredible. But how can I bring up the idea in a way that won't upset my girlfriend (I don't want her to think she's "not enough" for me!). And if she does agree, are there any ground rules we should stick to?

A: Full disclosure: I've never had a threesome, so I may not know what I'm talking about. But if I were to guess, I'd say as far as ground rules go, there are three: make sure your thirdsome (?) is consenting and legal (age-wise, not immigration-status-wise—undocumented people deserve random threesomes, too!). After that, I would make sure she is pro-choice. If a condom breaks and you accidentally get her pregnant, it would be good to know where she stands on abortion.

As for your girlfriend, why are you assuming that you're enough for her? Maybe it's her fantasy to have a threesome? Maybe she secretly planted the idea in your head without you knowing she's the one who really wants it? Either way, I think going into a threesome with a healthy amount of insecurity on your part is probably a good way to play it.

Q: I slipped and accidentally told a friend something super intimate and personal about sex with my girlfriend, and he told *his* girlfriend, and of course it eventually got back to mine. Now she's so mad she can barely look at me. How can I get myself out of the doghouse? And is it really so awful that I share stuff with a buddy?

A: What did you tell him? I want to know! Was it that she queefed in bed? That's not so bad. Everybody queefs—tell that gasbag to get over it! If it was something more serious, then I don't know what to tell you. You betrayed her trust; that's hard to come back from. I'm sure you've told her that you're sorry, but if words aren't working, maybe try telling her through actions. Buy her a dozen long-stemmed roses? If that's not enough, hire a mariachi band to serenade her (it would also support the mariachi economy, which I'm all for). If she hates mariachi and/or Mexican people, because maybe she's a Trump supporter, whisk her away on a tropical vacation (perhaps on Election Day, so that she doesn't vote). Or just tell her you won't do it again, and if you do and she breaks up with you, you'll learn your lesson for the next one.

Q: I'd like to get my girlfriend some really sexy underwear to wear in bed. Is that a good idea? And anything I should know or consider before I do it?

A: Part of me wants to advise you to just go for it, pick up whatever pair of underwear you deem sexy, buy it for her, and don't overthink it. Speaking of sexy underwear, have you heard of that period underwear Thinx? You could buy her that! I don't know what's sexier than underwear that you can menstruate all over (maybe a root canal?).

On the other hand, anytime you purchase something "sexy" for a woman, you are walking into a potential minefield (not because we're "difficult," but because our brains are more sophisticated than yours and we tend to read into things more often). What if you get her the wrong size? What if the underwear you buy was tried on by someone with some obscure STD that doesn't come out when washed, you end up transmitting it to your girlfriend, who then thinks you contracted it while cheating and gave it to her? There are so many ways this could play out! I wish I could talk from experience, but sadly, no man has ever bought me sexy underwear. I think it stems from the fact that deep down my suitors are afraid of me, and rightfully so. They know that any misstep will be judged and publicly ridiculed. I just learned so much about myself! But back to you: I guess the answer to this question lies in your girlfriend. You know what she likes; consider her tastes. If she wears lingerie, get her that. If like me, she doesn't wear lingerie because it's an oftentimes itchy, cheesy, expensive, uncomfortable relic of patriarchal oppression, get her something less loaded, like maybe an Amazon gift card.

Q: **My girlfriend is so loud during sex that the neighbors put a note under my door the next day asking us to keep it down. What should I do?**

A: I feel like you just wrote in to this column to overshare with us all the fact that your girlfriend is loud in bed.

Congratulations, dude, I'm so happy for you. But also be a good neighbor and tell your girlfriend to keep it down. Or, if you don't want to curb her sex sounds, then maybe just move somewhere remote like Appalachia, where people are so strung out on meth that your animal-like sex noises will fit right in! You could also cover your girlfriend's head with a pillow when she screams to muffle the sound, but be careful not to suffocate her. I don't want blood on my hands.

Q: **In movies I'm always seeing guys lifting a girl up and having sex up against a wall. They seem to be able to hold her up, get a great rhythm going, and stay at it for a long time. I've tried it, and I'm not all that good at it. Is there some trick I don't know about?**

A: There are a few factors here you need to consider: 1. It's Hollywood, so everything is an illusion. 2. There's probably a chair somewhere you don't see, or maybe a sad PA forced to kneel down while two body doubles bone atop him. 3. Consider the weight of the actress. Most real women aren't ninety pounds and thus are a little harder to lift. All that said, if you want to lift your partner, try strengthening your upper body by weight training or doing push-ups? Find a way to build muscle mass that doesn't involve steroids. Here's another option: hire someone stronger than you to fuck her and watch them do it.

Q: **If I meet an attractive woman at, say, a party, how do I flirt in a way that doesn't seem too aggressive** or sexual, but also shows that I'm interested in her? Flirting just doesn't come naturally to me!

A: The other sexperts may tell you to "make her laugh," but that only really works if you're cute. I'd like to believe most women respond to humor, but what we really respond to, at least right off the bat, is your appearance. If you are attractive, you can walk up to a woman and say pretty much anything short of "drink this" and we'll be swooning. If you aren't quite killing it in the looks department, you may need to employ your personality, and that's where humor can be an effective tool . . . unless she's also a comedian. As someone who tells jokes for a living, I tend to go for the misanthrope who tells me that the world's going to end or something equally apocalyptic and terrifying. Nothing gets my guard down more than thinking an asteroid is about to hit. But that's just me. If she's not a comic, humor is a safe default option. Maybe go up to her and tell her she looks like someone you know, sorry, someone you want to know! Get it? That's cute. Or tell her she looks under twenty-one and ask her to see her ID. Women love hearing that we look young—plus that way, you can find out if she's an organ donor. If she is an organ donor, maybe ask her if she really trusts that in the unfortunate event her life is on the line, some shady physician isn't going to pull the plug to harvest her organs. It's an edgy move but will get the conversation going.

Q: Our sex life has gotten a little boring, so I'm thinking of spicing it up by renting a hotel room for a night for a change of scenery. Is that a good idea or just sleazy? And any suggestions for things to do there—hot tub, rose petals in the bed . . . bondage?

A: I don't think a hotel room is sleazy. Then again, maybe sleazy is what she's into! So how about a motel instead? Bedbugs, black velvet oil painting of Elvis, gas station prosecco, other people's bodily fluids—what could be more romantic? You'll never know unless you try.

   Jokes aside, instead of worrying about your boring sex life, you should applaud yourself for sticking it out and still making an effort—most people leave relationships once they get a little stale, so that's a huge achievement! As far as other suggestions to spice things up, you could always steal a car, flee to Tijuana, inevitably get arrested by Mexican authorities, and land yourselves in a prison cell south of the border—I bet she'll give you points for the change of scenery!

Q: I think my girlfriend's reading my texts and emails on my phone—how can I find out? And please don't tell me to just ask her. I know she'll just get upset and say I don't trust her.

A: Well, it sounds like you don't trust her, but fine, don't be a mature adult and talk to her about it. . . . Let's have fun with this one. How about you text your most trusted friend something cool but also super specific about your girlfriend, like "I love when she makes me oatmeal chocolate chip coconut cookies," or "she's so cute when she sticks her pinky up my butt," and see how she responds. If you wake up to fresh-baked cookies and butt stuff, then you'll know the truth.

Q: I ran into an old girlfriend at the store the other night, and damn she looked good. Now I'm thinking maybe I was wrong to break up with her. Should I give it another go? If so, what's your advice for trying to re-spark a flame I willingly let go out a while ago?

A: First off, I'd like to start by saying thanks—for admitting you were wrong for breaking up with me, Kevin. And secondly, yes, I DO look great! After you bulldozed over my heart last July, I lost ten pounds and never gained it back. It was a little strange the other night, running into you, lingering in the self-help section at the feminist bookstore. Are you okay? You know what? That's none of my business. I'm in a really good place now and it's partly because I'm finally over you and in a way healthier relationship—with myself! I bet you didn't see that coming. See, Kevin, your apathetic attitude toward us brought out the worst in me. I have no hard feelings, though. If anything, your rejection helped me discover an inner strength I didn't know I had. But enough about me. If you're insistent on getting back together, like REALLY insistent, as you tend to be when you want something you can't have, I might just acquiesce out of sheer boredom or because you were the only guy who ever let me peg him. However, if I do decide to date you again, I will remind you every day we are together that I don't need you, I DON'T NEED YOU, KEVIN! Are we clear? I DON'T

NEED YOU! Also, can you pick up my mom from the airport?

Does dating that girl sound fun, Kevin, or whatever your name is? Still want to try to reignite a match soaked in your ex's tears? Go for it, but only if your heart is truly in the right place, and proceed with caution.

Bad Art

After my brief stint as a sex advice columnist, I was granted an opportunity to write a review for a friend's art publication. Having been on the receiving end of so much harsh criticism myself, I'm often loath to criticize another artist's work. But sometimes a "work" of "art" comes along that is so god-awful and so offensively bad, that it'd be a crime against humanity not to speak out against it. This is one of those times.

Jeff Koons' Blue Balls*

Otherwise known as epididymal hypertension, "blue balls" refer to the testicular pain that occurs after prolonged sexual stimulation without ejaculation. It's also a great way to describe Jeff Koons' current show at the Gagosian Gallery in Beverly Hills.

I should preface: I'm a fan of Jeff Koons. I have long admired his

---

* Originally published in Artnet.com

work (from the '80s) and even to this day, I appreciate the disdain he evokes from MFA grad students and other people I might walk away from at parties. In addition, I find his origin story immensely inspiring—rising from humble beginnings as a commodities broker at Smith Barney to becoming THE highest-paid visual artist of our time AND in an industry historically known to be nearly impossible for young, affluent, straight white men to break into. I mean, HOW does he not have a biopic already?!

On a personal note, Jeff Koons taught me that art could be anything—like someone else's art, a tax haven for the wealthy, or a tourist magnet to boost museum revenues. So it is with great sadness that I find myself writing anything even remotely negative about this purveyor of the provocative. But after spending what felt like many hours (forty-five minutes) gazing into Koons' blue balls, dangling over various reproductions of classical masterpieces, the only interpretation I could muster is that this whole series felt stale, lazy, and a bit inaccessible (but only because we couldn't find parking).

Take Koons' *Gazing Ball (Manet Luncheon on the Grass)*, for instance (materials include paint, a shit ton of assistants, and a metallic blue ball). It just made me want to see Manet's *Luncheon on the Grass*, only not obstructed by a metallic blue ball.

Or Koons' reproduction of the *Barberini Faun*, called *Gazing Ball (Barberini Faun)*. It would have been so much cooler if it were the actual *Barberini Faun* or any statue, for that matter, without a metallic blue ball on it.

There were a few other pieces that I'd probably neglect to mention if I weren't being paid by the word, like a shiny metallic balloon animal or a shiny metallic ballerina, which you could also happen upon in your run-of-the-mill Manhattan high-rise or on a handbag at H&M. But it's the blue balls that really rob the show.

Koons first exposed his balls in New York in 2013 and then again in 2015, on a knockoff of the *Mona Lisa*, probably because he knew she wouldn't tell. As I wandered around this current show, I kept wondering, why balls? Why violate other artists' work with balls when you could just do it with a dick? Or would that be too on the nose? I'm not a visual artist, but if I were Koons (apologies in advance), I'd purchase actual classical masterpieces (he can afford it), jerk off all over them (Pollock-style), and then sell those reproductions (pun intended) to idiots for millions. That's what I'd call balls!

Sorry, I got carried away. I don't want to shit on Jeff Koons (unless he pays me), but am I missing something? Am I not deep enough to appreciate what he's going for? I gazed into the orb for answers, but found none. Then I gazed at the gallery's press release, which read: "Each gazing ball reactivates and intensifies familiar scenes, whether from legend or the everyday." . . . Cool, that explains everything!

At one moment, as I stared at *Gazing Ball (David Intervention of the Sabine Women)*, I noticed a woman in the ball staring back at me. She was cute but judgmental, mid-thirties but definitely not yet past her prime. At first glance I thought she was a Sabine from the painting, but then after a longer gaze, I realized it was actually my own reflection, telling me it was time to leave.

I listened to the painting and fled at once. It was only a few minutes later, when I looked at Twitter (follow me at @jenafriedman!), that I realized something beautiful and profound about Jeff Koons' Gazing Ball series—it had taken my mind off of Trump! If for only a brief moment, I was consumed by the exorbitant mediocrity of

Koons' overpriced art/merch rather than the downfall of American democracy (apparently, my brain can only process one ostentatious relic of the '80s at a time). In any event, it was a welcomed and much-needed respite. So on that note, cheers to you, Mr. Koons! And to anyone who wants to be angry about something other than our government, go see his show!

Girl Having Sex, or,

What We Talk about When

We Talk about Likability

The first comedy manager I ever had told me that what makes or breaks a successful comedian is likability. He then dropped me for not being likable.

Naturally, I was devastated. I had only been doing stand-up for a few years, and I had no idea what likability meant or how I was supposed to exude it. The story has a happy ending, though; a few weeks later I got my first TV writing job, and since my manager had already dropped me, he missed out on the 10 percent commission—the joke's on you, Ari!*

So what is likability, anyway? According to my former manager, it's the capacity to generate work, to book paid gigs, and

---

*His name is Avi, but I thought it would be fun to pretend I forgot.

make him money. In the real world, likability is entirely subjective, but in entertainment, it's a little more quantifiable. In an industry where people are the product, likability is often just a euphemism for profitability. Do midwestern moms want to fuck them? Do Rust Belt dads want to drink a shitty beer with them? Does this person make other people want to pay attention to them, buy things from them, or spend money on them?

Growing up, I never cared about being likable. As a kid, if people didn't like me, it didn't bother me. It was only when I started working in comedy that I realized I needed to be likable in order to make a living. In an unregulated work environment with no HR department and no barriers to entry, so much of your success is based on your personal relationships. I knew I had to work hard and be funny, but I didn't anticipate how much I would also need to make people *like me* so they would give me opportunities to work hard and be funny.

Likability is also inextricably linked to gender and race. For white men, the likability formula is pretty clear-cut: as long as you're not a serial killer, you're likable. And even if you are a (white, male) serial killer, you'll probably still end up with a fan club, a Netflix special, and some hot, young goth chick who visits you in prison (and maybe has aspirations to turn your corpse into a tourist attraction after you die, but so what if she does? Girl's gotta eat!). But if you're a white *woman* or a person of color, likability is a little harder to come by. It's not just given to you because you stepped onstage wearing a tiny T-shirt that accentuates your dad bod (or guy curves?). You have to earn it.

When I first started performing stand-up comedy around 2005, I quickly became aware of how audiences saw me: as an unknown, young white woman onstage with her clothes on. When a

Chicago heckler screamed out, "Can I get a blow job?" in the middle of one of my first live performances, the mostly male audience laughed louder at his line than they had at any of mine. I was too inexperienced as a comic to shut him down with a joke, so I just thought, *Fuck it* and walked offstage.

I was at least likable enough offstage to get booked on that show, but likability offstage came with caveats. The booker, let's call him Ralph, was a mild-mannered guy who supported a lot of younger female comics on the Chicago scene at the time. I later learned that Ralph was also A REGISTERED SEX OFFENDER, a "reformed, harmless one" but a sex offender nonetheless. A decade earlier, he had been arrested for grabbing women's crotches without their consent (this was before such behavior was specifically forgiven by 61.9 million Americans in a federal election). When I was first starting out in stand-up, I ran into a lot of men like Ralph. If I hadn't been "liked" by them or worked in rooms they booked, I probably wouldn't have worked at all.

I wish I could say that I regret performing on Ralph's shows, but I don't. The irony is that he was actually nicer to me and to a lot of other women on the scene than many of the other male comedy bookers in Chicago back then. Also, the stage time Ralph gave me made me a better comic. I wish that I could say I've encountered fewer predators as I've advanced through the ranks of this industry, but that would be a lie. I now just have more power and agency to avoid them.

When the "like" button first appeared on social media, it had a democratizing effect. That anyone with a computer could be seen or heard or read at the click of a button leveled the playing field for a whole generation of young artists and other marginalized voices.

So much of my early career success can be traced to videos

that I made on my own or with friends and then uploaded onto YouTube. I once recorded a video where I played a naive woman smitten by an American-born jihadist, a real guy named Omar Hammami (RIP Omar), who had recently been profiled in the *New York Times*. In the clip, I fantasized over meeting a man who had such perfectly chiseled cheekbones and was wanted by the FBI. I called the digital love letter "Jihad Me at Hello" and posted it on YouTube.

By the next morning the video had accumulated thousands of likes, the 2010 version of going viral. When I read the comments, I was surprised to discover that many people who watched my performance thought it was real. Apparently, it seemed more likely that the girl in the video would have a crush on an aspiring terrorist than a satirical point of view. I was thrilled that I'd finally made something that people enjoyed, so I called my mom to share the good news. But when she watched "Jihad Me at Hello," she did not "like" it. In fact, she hated it. She called me back in tears and begged me to remove it from YouTube.

But the clip caught the attention of a manager who got the joke and signed me as a client. While that relationship didn't last long (see above), I didn't need it to. The internet allowed me to carve out my own path and not rely on traditional channels or antiquated notions of how likable I needed to be in order to be successful. Off-line, as I got better at stand-up and got booked by sex offenders who weren't yet registered, I started to find ways to make live audiences like me.

I remember performing on a midnight show at the Comedy Store in London—a venue notoriously inhospitable to unknown acts. When the host announced my name, the entire front row cleared to refill their drinks. The flood of people was so apparent that it actually generated laughs among the remaining crowd before I even got to my first line. I eventually won the room over with some (literal) dick jokes that I had prepared in advance in the event that I might need them.

I quickly learned that one surefire way to make all audiences like me was by telling dirty jokes. After all, sex sells, and nothing is more of a universal crowd-pleaser than a dick joke. In a few years, I would develop an aversion to joking about dicks and sex in my stand-up, but only because it was starting to feel like those jokes were becoming my only option.

It occurs to me that a lot of female comics, when we're first starting out in stand-up, are encouraged to talk about our sex lives onstage because it's the only way we can get men to listen. As I got older and my comedy evolved, it began to feel like a radical act *not* to talk about sex onstage and not give in to the male fantasy of being a fly on the wall of a women's locker room. I started to challenge myself to ditch the blue humor and joke about things like politics instead, and long story short, that's why nobody knows me!*

• • •

It wasn't just onstage that sex comedy often felt like my quickest path toward likability (and actually being paid for my work). Most of the acting roles I was invited to audition for when I was first starting out were one-dimensional parts that almost always involved nudity and were almost always written by men.

Even after I signed to one of the most reputable comedy management companies in Hollywood, my first call to audition came for the role of "Girl Having Sex" in a major studio comedy.

---

* Self-deprecating comedy is LIKABLE!

From: REDACTED

Date: Tue, 21 Sep 2010 13:14:31-0700

To: Jena Friedman

CC: REDACTED

Subject: Jena Friedman / REDACTED audition

Dear Jena,

Are you interested in doing this audition? Please let us know.

*PLEASE NOTE: ACTRESS MUST BE COMFORTABLE WITH NUDITY (there will be no nudity necessary for the audition but please be aware that the role requires nudity)

Date: Wednesday, September 22

Time: 10:45am

Location: REDACTED

With: REDACTED

Project: REDACTED because these people are still WORKING!

Role: [GIRL HAVING SEX] female, 20s, having sex at a rocking party and is interrupted by Noah who is looking for his girlfriend . . . **ACTRESS MUST BE COMFORTABLE WITH NUDITY**

Prepare: SEE BELOW

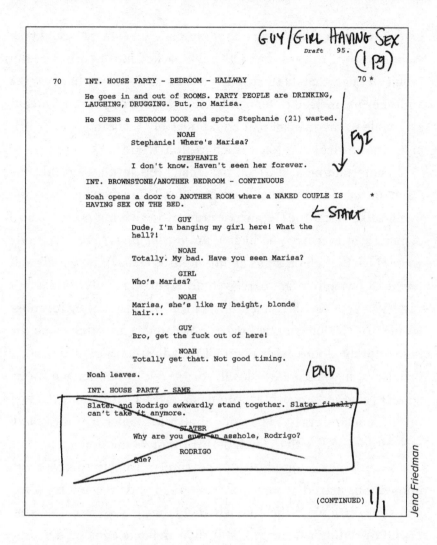

When I received the email inviting me to audition to play a nameless, topless woman with one line in a major motion picture, I was kind of flattered that someone even considered me, since breast size is one of my least distinguishing characteristics. But I was equally disappointed that my reps thought it would be a good idea to put me up for such a lame role. At the same time, I was submitting writing packets to work on late-night comedy shows, and

I wasn't sure that humping a random dude on camera would be a stepping-stone toward that. I also felt backed into a corner by the inquiry. I knew that if I turned down the audition, I might never get another one. Instead of being likable, which in this context meant agreeable to my managers, I could possibly be branded as "difficult," the scarlet letter for women in Hollywood.

In entertainment, difficult is actually the antithesis to likable. Someone can be so unlikable to the point where they then become likable, like Oscar the Grouch or Fran Lebowitz, but no one who's difficult can ever become likable. In *Just the Funny Parts*, comedy writer Nell Scovell presents an unscientific chart of how male and female showrunners are perceived differently in Hollywood. For a variety of actions, like "defending a joke" or "negotiating for more money" or "hiring friends," male showrunners are often given the benefit of the doubt, with a panoply of adjectives ascribed to their behaviors, like "creative," "loyal," or "savvy," while female show-runners who act similarly are often perceived as "difficult," "crazy," or "difficult and crazy." The same applies to women in positions all over Hollywood, with the notable exception of missionary.

When I was granted the "opportunity" to audition to be an anonymous naked woman on camera, I didn't want to come across as difficult to the men who held the keys to my career success. I also didn't want to insult their delicate egos by deriding any of their "creative strategic choices." I spent so much energy crafting the email that would allow me to lightly duck out of the audition without sounding strident or difficult.

From: JENA FRIEDMAN (ME!)
Sent: Tuesday, September 21, 2010 5:58 PM
To: REDACTED VERY POWERFUL HOLLYWOOD MANAGER

CC: REDACTED JUNIOR MANAGERS WHO ARE NOW
   POWERFUL HOLLYWOOD MANAGERS
Subject: w: Jena Friedman / REDACTED audition

Hey! Totally thankful for the audition, but it also made me
realize that we haven't talked about what types of roles we all
think I should be going out for (nudity, sex, etc.), perhaps we
could discuss later this week? As I mentioned, I'm out all day
tomorrow for a funeral, but I could talk thurs or friday if you're
available, thanks!—Jena

Sent on the Sprint® Now Network from my BlackBerry®

It didn't work.* The management company dropped me and my
BlackBerry soon after.

• • •

I've wasted a lot of time trying to chase down the white whale of likability. If only I realized then what I know now: misogyny, even in its most subtle form, makes likability for many women a pipe dream.

I once overheard a booker of a highly respected comedy festival admit that he would "tune out" anytime he saw a female comic walk onstage wearing high-heeled boots (i.e., "fuck-me boots" . . . what's not funny about fuck-me boots?!). I knew that the booker's comment was off base and sexist, but it still got into my head. In fact, I thought of it every single time I auditioned after that. Even as my material became increasingly feminist, I wasted hours sort-

---

*I didn't even get pity points for the real funeral, which I really did attend that week.

ing out what to wear onstage so that no asshole in the audience could look at me and just "tune out."

A year later, when I auditioned in front of that same booker for a place on his new talent showcase, I made sure to wear sneakers. But even though my set went great and my material was killer, I didn't secure a spot in the festival. Only two of the sixteen available spots went to women that year. It was only after I heard countless other stories from other female comics regarding this same booker that I realized maybe the problem wasn't our shoes. Likability feels pretty far in the distance, when a woman's worth can be reduced to her taste in footwear.

• • •

I think I stopped caring about being likable when I turned thirty. Around that time, I wrote my first hour show, *American Cunt*, which was an ode to not being likable. I performed the show at the Edinburgh Fringe Festival to mostly positive reviews. Since the show was in part a celebration of unlikability, the likable reviews only pushed me further to explore the space my new freedom had granted me. The following is one such joke.

> *I want to start dating women but I'm not attracted to women, so how do I go about that? Do I just start by dating men shorter than me?*
> [THE AUDIENCE GROANS]
> *I knew you wouldn't like that! That joke was not in the show originally, but I got some reviewers saying "she's edgy" and "she pulls no punches." You wanna know what's edgy? Not jokes about AIDS, rape, Ebola, or abortion . . . but joking about men shorter than me! That is the last frontier: you do not*

joke about short men! YOU DO NOT JOKE ABOUT SHORT
MEN!!!!

Why not? (A) Because that's who runs shit. (B) I look to
the women in the audience for support, and you can't laugh
because that's who you're here with! Short men are the keepers.

Don't feel bad for short men, boo-hoo, being born with
a will to succeed. Sorry, I want to set the record straight. I
actually don't see gender—once it's below my eyeline.

In 2015 a tallish female making fun of short men was a clear violation of the likability contract that I had established and refined over the years with my PC, body-positive, hipster audience. It was the one topic that I knew I wouldn't be able to get away with unless I broke the fourth wall and made the joke about how I couldn't get away with joking about short men.

Months after the taped special of the show came out online, I received an email on February 14 (so perhaps a Valentine?) from a guy who was offended by that joke and decided to share his feelings with me. To protect his identity, I've changed his name to Napoleon:

Dear Jena,

My name is Napoleon. I'm a Junior undergrad student at [redacted university], majoring in the Department of Gender, Women and Sexuality Studies. . . .

I am short for a man at 5'5". . . . However, I would prefer to think that my height is not a shortcoming, not a flaw, and not something that defines me or places me within a category.

In your stand-up you suggest that dating a short man would be the equivalent of dating a woman. Is that because you see women as being "small"? . . . It has been made clear to me that the feminist movement aims to break down old, tired, conservative gender stereotypes and it challenges constructed ideologies that create pressure to conform or measure up to unrealistic beauty standards and expectations. That said, can you please explain your joke about short men? Are you suggesting that a man under a certain measurement in height is not a real man? . . .

More importantly, there will be young people searching the internet in support of their height, only to find someone (cool like you) telling them that being short (which can't be changed) is not worthy. . . . it's not edgy, it's not funny. That is what's known as bullying.

Thank you for your time.

—Napoleon

Poor kid. I feel for him, but what he lacked in height, he also lacked in sense of humor. He also proved me right: jokes about short men are a no-go! I had never received such an in-depth dissertation—I mean email—about a joke before, and I didn't know what to make of it. Did this mean that I had arrived? Was I now finally so likable onstage that even though some guy didn't appreciate a joke in my show, he still felt comfortable enough to email me his thoughts about it? Either way, at least it wasn't a dick pic.

• • •

It was hard for me to tour *American Cunt* across the US because even the most open-minded cities (Doug Fir Lounge in Portland, Oregon, I'm talking to you) wouldn't put the title of the show on their marquee. But I loved that title, and people's reactions to it made me want to defend it even more. No word in the English language is more connected to female likability, or the lack thereof, than the word "cunt." A term of endearment in the UK, a sexist slur in the US, cunt is literally just another word for vagina. But the "c-word" is also apparently the greatest insult one could call a woman, according to men. A male journalist once told me that "cunt" is "the least likable word anyone could call a woman." When I disagreed, he doubled down, insisting that no word in the English language is more insulting to the female gender! I calmly replied, "I actually just wrote a whole show on the word 'cunt,' and it's far less insulting than being called—"

"You're crazy!" he cackled, completing my sentence. With no self-awareness, this legit journalist hurled at me the most insidious c-word one could call a woman: crazy. The irony is that him calling me crazy made my case more than anything my shrill voice could have mustered.

Whereas "cunt" is a harsh word that reflects even more poorly on the person stating it than its target, "crazy" is an erasure. It mutes its victim. It denies the cunt a voice. This was just one of the many insights I turned into jokes throughout my hour-long meditation on gender and likability.

Chaucer used the word "cunt." So did James Joyce, Samuel Beckett, D. H. Lawrence. So many great men throughout history have used the word "cunt," and I am sure women would have, too, if we had been taught how to read.

I continued touring *American Cunt*, refining portions of it and updating jokes to match the 2016 election cycle, which was now in full swing. What better time to be joking about likability and gender than in the run-up to Hillary Clinton's anointment as our nation's first female president? It turns out a girl can dream ... but that dream may never become a reality.*

• • •

The election of Donald Trump proved that likability in America is inextricably linked to male power. After all, what does it take to get elected other than likability? Apparently nothing.

For months, I tried to understand what perfect storm led to Donald Trump becoming the leader of the free world. I even wrote a satirical recipe on what I believed the ingredients to be.

Shouts & Murmurs

(January 9, 2017 issue of the *New Yorker*)

A Recipe

BY JENA FRIEDMAN

With the Inauguration almost upon us, I thought I'd share an old family recipe, of Italian origin, passed down to my grandmother from her aunt in Germany. The ingredients have been tweaked to appeal to American tastes.

Warning: This dish contains nuts.

---

*But who knows, by the time you read this, maybe Kamala will be president?

INGREDIENTS:

- ¼ of all eligible voters (or less, depending on how many votes you can suppress)
- 1 charismatic leader with a wildly successful book, TV show, or film (and weird facial or head hair)
- 1 gaggle of Russian hackers
- 1 well-timed WikiLeak
- 1 rogue F.B.I. director (or other high-level government official)
- A dollop of racism
- A spritz of anti-Semitism
- A sprinkle of idiocy (for a low-fat version, substitute applesauce for idiocy)
- The media

PREPARATION:

1. Preheat the planet to record temperatures to accelerate climate change, and trigger a global refugee crisis. Put the refugee crisis aside and let it rise. It will come into play later.

2. Next, you'll need a melting pot, or the illusion of one. Mix a colorful figure (preferably orange) into a liberal but fractured democracy, where the left has been weakened by infighting and the right has been reduced by impotent leadership.

   Note: The figure may curdle the dish, unless he appears at first to be a joke, a clown, or a total idiot. Add the media here to help emulsify.

3. Allow the mixture to congeal into a malignant orange mass, and let it stew in the pot for several months, heating the populace

with racist rhetoric. Now that the refugee crisis has risen, knead it back into the mixture, along with any leftover xenophobia, bigotry, or fears of terrorism lying around in your cupboard.

Note: This recipe calls specifically for Islamic terrorism. Even a small splash of domestic terrorism (often a by-product of toxic masculinity and lax gun laws) will sour the mix, so store your terrorisms separately.

4. As for misogyny, a little goes a long way. It's already everywhere, like salt or CO_2 emissions, so there's no need to overdo it. But, if you do have a taste for it, you can spice up the dish with a pinch of ass, a small handful of pussy, a smear of telling a candidate who has spent forty years in public service that she looks tired, or a scant cup of sexual-assault accusers paraded around as human shields on live TV. (Fun tip: Add insult to injury by not paying for their hair and makeup!)

Note: If accusers start to bubble up in the pot, put a lid on it immediately by enlisting the F.B.I. director to do something moronic to deflect from snowballing sexual-assault allegations.

5. At this point, everything may begin to boil over. Common sense would call for lowering the temperature, but that would obscure the full, rich (or ostensibly rich, but who really knows without tax returns) flavor. Instead, toss in some outside help to keep the concoction heated but contained, like a D.N.C. hack or another variety of Russian cyber-terrorism (e.g., tampering with voter databases), as no one you are serving will seem to notice these extra ingredients.

Note: To prevent progressives from sticking together, whisk some yolks into the mix. The kids will think it's béarnaise and eat it right up!

6. Whip the ingredients into a pungent, gravy-like sludge. The early admixture of the media (including social media) will insure the perfect sludginess.

7. Once it seems edible, serve on Election Day. Be advised, however, that this recipe is not meant to appeal to all tastes; in fact, most Americans have never been exposed to this dish and probably won't be able to stomach it, but as long as they don't vote (or aren't able to, thanks to the repeal of key provisions of the Voting Rights Act), your dinner should be a hit!

Yield: Serves 10–12, mostly Trumps but not Tiffany.

It was infuriating to watch one of the most accomplished female candidates of her generation, or maybe ever, run neck and neck with a racist sexual predator. Yet as I witnessed the sexism of the campaign on full display, I was loath to blame it on Hillary's gender, because playing the gender card would be . . . unlikable! A few days before I was to tape my special, I finally figured out the perfect joke that encapsulated how I felt.

America has more words for why we hate Hillary than Inuits have for snow, but it's not because she's a woman, right? If you ask people why they hate her, they'll say it's because she's unlikable, inauthentic, a cunt . . . but they'll never say it's because she's a woman—

So maybe we'll never know.

If only there was a way to gauge American misogyny. You'd have to conduct a social experiment where you could put Hillary up against the worst candidate known to mankind … you see where this is going? Someone so sexist and racist that he seemed like a joke, a guy who was such a threat to national security that even borderline sexists and racists would find him offensive. Run that guy against Hillary and see how he does, and then and only then would you ever get a sense of what percent of America would rather see a tweeting asteroid crash into our democracy than a woman lead it.

Love her or hate her, here was a woman who worked her entire life to conform to society's expectations of how likable she needed to be in order to be accepted, only to lose to a clown in the end. But in the aftermath of that traumatizing election, something cool happened: women everywhere stopped giving a shit about being likable.

• • •

In 2019, I previewed a new hour show, *Miscarriage of Justice,* at the Edinburgh Fringe Festival. I had been working on the show for over a year, and I had a lot to say. It was definitely a polarizing hour of comedy, and it was a lot darker than my first show. I talked about violence against women, the #MeToo movement (I'm sure it has long escaped our cultural consciousness by now, so feel free to google it), mass shootings, domestic terrorism, and the rise of fascism, among other topics a little light on LOLs. I wasn't sure how it was going to land in Edinburgh, since regional political humor sometimes gets lost in translation. But I knew that performing the show over twenty-six consecutive nights to an international audience would only make it better.

Since there are over three thousand live shows at the Edinburgh Fringe Festival, reviewers are critical in helping audiences determine which shows to pay attention to and which to ignore. A glowing write-up from the right publication can make the industry take notice and catapult an artist's career.

In 2017 a female blogger by the name of Jay Jay (I never thought I would write this sentence, either), who was quoted on the online comedy website Chortle,* reported that 69 percent of Edinburgh Fringe Festival shows that year were reviewed by men, and the star ratings performers were given that year reflected that gender disparity. Male reviewers were writing more favorable reviews for male performers than for their female counterparts. In one of the most reputable festival publications, the *Scotsman*, the gender bias was stark.

> All eight of the newspaper's five-star comedy reviews were for men, while sixty percent of its two-star reviews and three of the four one-star reviews were for women, even though they represented only 32 percent of the acts reviewed.

When I debuted my show in Edinburgh, the reviews I received reflected a similar bias. Of the twelve publications that reviewed my show in 2019, I received four five-star reviews. Two were from women and two were from men (neither of the men were straight and white). I also received five four-star reviews, three from

---

*UNCREDITED! "Are Edinburgh Fringe Reviewers Sexist?" Chortle, September 5, 2017.

women and one from a straight white guy (#progress). The rest of the reviews were all three-star reviews, all from (presumably) straight, white, British men. I could have chalked it up to coincidence or my own inability to resonate with a certain demographic of Edinburgh critic, but it seemed like something else was at play. It wasn't in the star ratings as much as in the words certain male critics used to interpret female artists' work. Courtney Pauroso is an incredibly brilliant comedian and clown who performed a groundbreaking show in Edinburgh the year that I was there. I still feel lucky to have seen it live. When I read a review of her show in the *Guardian*, in which a male critic called her "the latest sexy clown from Dr. Brown [Courtney's mentor]," I wondered if that same reviewer had ever called a male comic sexy or given credit to a male comic's mentor in the opening line of a review for his show.

With twenty or so live performances remaining in my run, I thought this observation might make interesting comedic fodder to talk about onstage. I began to incorporate the reviews of my performance into the performance itself. Take this excerpt from a three-star review in the *Scotsman*.

> Satirically cutting-edge, frequently brutal, you could isolate any number of Friedman's lines and marvel at their elegant, rapier wit. . . . But by opening up more, sugaring the bitter pills ever so slightly, she'd be an almighty force to be reckoned with.

What did he mean by "opening up more"? Smiling more, sharing details about my personal life, spreading my legs onstage (to be fair, I probably should have done that)? When I read the review, I marveled at the critic's use of the adjective "rapier" to describe my wit. The critic, let's call him Wanker, had just sat through an hour show about sexism, misogyny, rape, and THE POWER OF WORDS, and the first word that came to his mind to describe it was "rapier." It was kind of funny. The joke about his review practically wrote itself:

I didn't want to make fun of the reviewer with my rapier *wit . . . but he was ASKING FOR IT.*

Turning the reviewer into the reviewed made me feel powerful. It gave me a sense of control over my work, which was being dissected by a demographic I didn't write it for. It also allowed me to do what comedians do best, critique the culture that we're in— which at that time was an international monthlong festival where a white, heterosexual, British male majority got to dictate whose voices would be heard.

A week later, I received my first review from a female critic, named Ellis Lee. She wrote for a student publication called *Fresh Air*. Her words reaffirmed why I wrote the show in the first place and renewed my faith in it. Thanks to her five-star review alone, I was able to sell out the rest of my run and actually make some money off the show. I am tempted to post the whole thing here, but that would be . . . unlikable! I'm not just saying that—it's been studied. Women who acknowledge their achievements are statistically viewed as less likable among their colleagues.[*]

• • •

---

[*] Stéphanie Thomson, "A Lack of Confidence Isn't What's Holding Back Working Women," *The Atlantic*, September 20, 2018, https://www.theatlantic.com/family/archive/2018/09/women-workplace-confidence-gap/570772/.

As empowering as it is not to care about being liked, it doesn't always pay. But then again, for so many women who do stand-up comedy, few things do pay!

In 2019 I took *Miscarriage of Justice* to the New York Comedy Festival, where I was also asked to participate in an unpaid "women in the industry" panel discussion. I'm always game to pontificate on unpaid panels, because I do believe having the uncomfortable conversations in public spaces is how we evolve.

When I arrived at the event, I noticed cameras everywhere. Perhaps I hadn't read the fine print, but no one had informed me that the panel discussion was being filmed, let alone in front of an obnoxiously large Citigroup banner as part of the bank's gender equity initiative.

A Citigroup rep met me at the door with a contract and asked me to sign my name on it in order to participate on the panel. When I scanned the agreement briefly, I saw that it granted permission for the global finance behemoth to "license the panelist's likeness in perpetuity" . . . for free. "Yeah right," I chuckled to myself at the insane request, and politely declined to sign it.

Apparently, I was the only panelist who wouldn't sign the release form. Was I being DIFFICULT, or was it just that no one else had read the contract? As a field producer, it was often my job to spring contracts on unassuming subjects prior to filming, so I tend to exercise more caution than most when signing anything where I'll be on camera. But in an effort to placate the comedy festival (who I assume must have had a financial arrangement with the bank), and be likable (just this once), I said that I would be happy to participate, but I would not sign the contract. The representative reluctantly accepted my request and moved me to a seat on the end of the panel, so that the cameras could cut around me. It seemed like a fair compromise.

As the panel commenced, the moderator asked all the women a question to break the ice: "What's the naughtiest thing you've ever done?" She giggled. Jesus fucking Christ. Seriously? There was a list of preapproved questions we'd been sent, and this was not one of them. Normally, I would just laugh it off like everyone else on the panel did, but that day I was tired. Would any moderator dare ask this same question to a group of professional men? Would there even have been a panel of male comedy executives and producers discussing gender inequality in the entertainment industry, being that they are often the ones who propagate it?*

I was tired and I was annoyed. I was annoyed that the event was branded without being paid. I was annoyed that the bank was filming us without having asked in advance. I was annoyed that the moderator opened the conversation with a dumb question about our personal lives, but I also recognized that she only did it because she knew a question like that would get the crowd quiet, since the weight of our accomplishments apparently couldn't. I was annoyed that I had to speak on the panel in the first place, that I couldn't just do my show in the festival like so many of the male comics got to do, that I also had to agree to participate in this branded fake feminist initiative as well. I was annoyed that there was so much inequality on a panel about inequality, and I was annoyed that I was the one who was going to have to call it out.

When it came time for me to answer the question, I abandoned any pretense of likability. "What's the naughtiest thing I've ever

---

*There are a lot of female asshole gatekeepers in our business, too!

done?" I said dryly. "Not sign Citigroup's release form to be on this unpaid panel." The audience audibly gasped. Did my snarky comment go too far? Did I even care?

The answer was no to both.

One good thing did come out of that silly panel. I made a friend! The insanely talented *New Yorker* cartoonist Hilary Fitzgerald Campbell was seated next to me that day, and we bonded over our shared frustration at being unwitting shills for a global bank's unpaid gender equity initiative. After leaving the panel, she even drew a cartoon inspired by it (see below). She's never published it anywhere, but she was kind enough to let me include it here. Not only is it hilarious, it's the perfect segue to the next chapter of this book. Thanks, Hilary!

"What's it like to be a male, in a male-dominated field?"

Hilary Fitzgerald Campbell

• • •

Toward the end of *The Likeability Trap*, journalist Alicia Menendez's book on likability and the challenges it poses for women in the workplace, Menendez writes, "A woman can alter her approach to likability but she is subject to penalty if the world around her does not change as well." She's right, and I'll probably never be invited to perform in the New York Comedy Festival again. But the good news is that the world around us is changing, slowly and in part thanks to people, including so many countless, often unrecognized women and nonbinary folks, forcing society to change.

Recently, I was offered a small part in a movie, which I said yes to immediately, before actually reading the script (never do that), because I was a fan of the lead actor. That afternoon, when I read my lines and noticed that my character had a sex scene, I kind of freaked out. I really didn't want to be a bit character in a movie where I humped a guy on camera, just like I hadn't wanted to do it a decade prior. At least this time the part was clothed and I didn't have to audition for it, but still. I called my agent and backed out of the role. This time, my reps happened to be women; they understood my reservations and supported my decision to back out of the project.*

But then something unexpected happened. The creative team behind the movie wanted to know why I didn't want the part. How was I supposed to respond without coming across as a difficult, sex-negative prude (which also may be the name of my next solo show)? My agent said she'd deal with any negative fallout and that

---

*I have some really great male reps now, too!

143

the producers wouldn't hold it against me. When my agent told the film's producers that I wasn't comfortable with the sex scene, the male director and male lead actor and female producer responded in the coolest possible way: they invited me to brainstorm ideas to rewrite it. What?! Really?? That never happens. I was floored. It was a dream scenario. I pitched a few sex scenes that I thought could work, that didn't involve me physically humping anyone, and we all agreed to give them a try. In the end, we landed on a really funny and creative scene that functioned just as well as the original. Plus, I could rest easy knowing that it wouldn't freak out my parents.

This anecdote may not seem like a big deal from the outside, but to me it really was. The subtly misogynistic and overtly sexist comedy that was ubiquitous in Hollywood back when I was invited to audition to be Girl Having Sex was being phased out, and it was no longer DIFFICULT to say I was uncomfortable humping someone on camera. It didn't just feel like I had "arrived," it felt like mainstream consciousness of how to portray women—even in the raunchiest comedies—was shifting ever so slightly in a positive direction. The movie went on to be a tremendous success, and the experience reaffirmed my faith in the best aspects of the comedy industry and its openness to evolve. I could have just as easily been told to go fuck off, as I had been many times before, but I wasn't. Instead, I was listened to and trusted to come up with something funny, all because I didn't care about being likable.

And what's more likable than that?

Brief Interviews with Hilarious Men

f I had a dollar for every time a journalist asked me, "Is it hard being a woman in comedy?" I'd probably make as much as a man in comedy.

The truth is, being a woman in comedy is fine, and sometimes it's really great. I have nothing to compare it to. It comes with the same indignities as being a woman in almost every other industry in America, but at least we have a microphone!

There is, however, one aspect of the job that's pretty annoying: constantly fielding inane, distracting, and sexist questions during press interviews. If only we could all just do our work and answer questions about that, but no. So often, female comics have to answer questions about anything else: from sexism in society to our male coworkers' sexual misconduct allegations. It makes me wonder if male comedians ever get similar questions from journalists, and if so, how do they respond when asked them?

Inspired by all the batshit-crazy but completely real questions that I and other female comedians have endured over the years from legitimate journalists (including notable ones from publications such as the *Guardian*, the *New Yorker*, and the *New York Times*), I asked my favorite male comedians the most sexist (but 100 percent real) questions that I could find, mostly verbatim, just with the genders reversed.

The results were illuminating.

A little note on my methodology: For all my interviews, I reached out to my favorite male comedian friends and mentors. I prefaced my intent in advance (something I rarely do before interviews). Each interview was done individually, via phone or email, but everyone got similar questions. Some responses are verbatim, while others are condensed for clarity.

What's it like to be a man in comedy?

JON STEWART: [laughs] It's golden. Basically, men in comedy are carried into the clubs. It's incredibly pampering, you're paid in Dogecoin—did I even say that right? Dogecoin and cocaine futures.

EUGENE MIRMAN: Um, you know, it feels fine. It feels like I have opportunities I can pursue [laughs]—I'm sorry you get that question. It's so outside of what I do that it really makes it clear that interviews for you are probably unpleasant.

JENA FRIEDMAN: This is just the first one!

BOB ODENKIRK: Uh . . . perfectly uninteresting, un-unique. It's, uh . . . what's it like being a man in comedy? I fit right in [laughs].

JENA FRIEDMAN: You're doing great. It doesn't have to be funny—

BOB ODENKIRK: I'm allowed to be a crude asshole and get laughs from it and let that part of my psyche out in a public way for the sake of laughter.

PATTON OSWALT: Sometimes the road can be a little rough. I don't want to make it sound like some horror movie, but sometimes club owners are more concerned with drink sales and not focused on, say, crowd control. And then there's that double-edged sword of, "I could use a little support here," but then you're ALSO like, "Men can take care of themselves." There's still a long way to go, but it's fun.

JIM GAFFIGAN: Well, I can't really speak for my entire gender.

REGGIE WATTS: [really long pause]

JENA FRIEDMAN: Reggie?

REGGIE WATTS: Yes.

JENA FRIEDMAN: Is it hard to be a man in comedy?

REGGIE WATTS: It is, because you constantly have to watch your back, you have to make sure what people are laughing at are your jokes and not just your nice hips.

When did you decide to become a male comedian?

EUGENE MIRMAN: [laughing] I can't handle that, uh, that it's, that—anyway, I guess when I was eighteen I decided to be a male comedian. Or at seventeen I think I realized that comedy was the kind of job and I was male and so that's what happened.

JIM GAFFIGAN: Well, I didn't decide to become male. I was born male.

BOB ODENKIRK: I've always been male ... and I ... just ... WHAT?! [laughing] I always wanted to be a comedian since I ... I just did ... that is what I did. Yeah, uh ... yeah ... Since I was a kid. I always just ... [long pause] I didn't think I had a choice to become a female comedian, so ... it was a different time, I didn't have that option [laughing].

REGGIE WATTS: Uh, I was a little nervous about it at first because there's not a lot of precedent for male comedians. Age sixteen was when I started, but I probably did it for realsies when I was thirty years old.

FRED ARMISEN: [laughs] I think I was around thirty-two. It wasn't that much of a decision. I just started doing comedy more and more.

JON STEWART: [laughs] Um, you know for years I was a boy comedian, and I think it was at some point after my bar mitzvah that I decided—actually, I don't think I decided, I think it was just pronounced and anointed. It was at a ceremony—[beep] HOLY FUCK ... Could you hear that?

JENA FRIEDMAN: No, what?

JON STEWART: [is driving a car during the interview] You didn't hear that? All of a sudden an Amber Alert went off on my phone and made a shrieking noise—apparently there is a gentleman in a silver car in East Orange who is considered armed and dangerous and I have apparently been deputized to go get him.

JENA FRIEDMAN: Are you gonna end this interview so

you can find a missing child? That would be the best PR move. . . .

JON STEWART: Here's how important this interview is for me: you're just gonna go on a ride-along. I'm not going to end it, you're just going to experience *Cops*, Stew style. I can't believe you didn't hear that.

JENA FRIEDMAN: I love the idea that there's a B story to this interview [laughing].

Was it hard to be a male comedian back when you were starting out?

JON STEWART: [laughs] It's so interesting that they view it as a subspecies. Now to [journalists'] somewhat credit, it was actually much harder to be a female comedian when I started. It really was all men. There was Joy Behar, Susie Essman, there were some young comics, Laura Kightlinger, Janeane Garofalo, but they were sort of on the vanguard. But if you went to the Comedy Cellar on a Friday or Saturday night, it was mostly 100 percent male or 90 percent—

JENA FRIEDMAN: So to circle back to my question, was it harder to be a male comedian?

JON STEWART: [laughs] Right. Yes! Because the competition was fierce! There was only every slot, so you had to fight for all of them.

FRED ARMISEN: It wasn't that hard. I just didn't have many expectations. You know, even if I performed to not many people, it was fun for me anyway.

Do you think it has changed for men since you got into the business?

EUGENE MIRMAN: Yeah.

JENA FRIEDMAN: In what ways?

EUGENE MIRMAN: YouTube.

REGGIE WATTS: I think men have more to worry about, and that's a good thing. It's nice to see advancements like that, in my lifetime.

FRED ARMISEN: I think everything has changed for everybody. Time just does that. But it's a good thing, things changing.

PATTON OSWALT: I think people are coming in with less expectations—they're not assuming you're going to talk about tools or cars or home repairs. Men go shopping, too!

JON STEWART: Definitely it has changed for us, when we finally broke through and were allowed in every comedy club . . . before men were allowed in comedy clubs, it was only men.

JIM GAFFIGAN: I don't understand where that question is coming from.

Do you think men can be attractive and funny?

EUGENE MIRMAN: Probably.

FRED ARMISEN: That's actually a good question, not that the other ones weren't good questions [laughs]. Yes, I do . . . Bob Odenkirk, he's attractive . . . I mean, Charlie Chaplin was attractive—

JENA FRIEDMAN: [laughs] Everyone's attractive to you.

JIM GAFFIGAN: I think they are two separate things, which really have nothing to do with one another. Funny is the only important thing in stand-up. Well, it should be, in my opinion.

JON STEWART: I have not seen it. I think if they were attractive, they wouldn't need to be funny.

Do you think men can be sexy and funny?

PATTON OSWALT: I'm not gonna lie and say that a nice shoulder-to-hips ratio doesn't open some doors, but after that, you'd better be able to deliver the material. You'd better be funny. I know a lot of male comedians who were VERY handsome and figured they could coast on that, but then Pepitone is suddenly getting all the TV gigs. It's a wake-up call once you hit that stage.

BOB ODENKIRK: Actually, no. I don't think comedians can be sexy. I suppose there might be a few who are, only to fetish freaks. I think part of being a comedian is being an underdog . . . not being cool, or sexy . . . I've always thought you can't have both, to be funny, you have to be making fun of convention. Beauty and sexiness is very often fitting an ideal.

JENA FRIEDMAN: These are all questions female comics have been asked, so if any are off-putting, I'm sorry.

BOB ODENKIRK: Tough shit is what you're saying [laughs].

Do you think it's more difficult for male comics who are not attractive?

JIM GAFFIGAN: Wait, are you saying I'm not . . .

JON STEWART: [laughs] Yes. It is very, very difficult. That's why we are out at night. I'm pretty sure that's why there's a two-drink minimum, it's not to loosen people up for the funny, it's to make us palatable to the eye.

REGGIE WATTS: It is, 100 percent. I have a lot of male friends who are not attractive, and they have lost out on many gigs, even open mics.

JENA FRIEDMAN: Are you being serious?

REGGIE WATTS: No, [laughs] no, I'm not.

FRED ARMISEN: I think for male comics who are not attractive, they'll find their place. And sometimes, they'll even make jokes about it . . . and by "they," I'm not implying that I think I'm attractive—[laughs]

JENA FRIEDMAN: [laughs] You're clearly on your toes by this line of questioning. Which is all I am really trying to achieve—

FRED ARMISEN: These are great.

JENA FRIEDMAN: They're all real questions.

FRED ARMISEN: God.

Is it harder to date since you've started doing stand-up?

REGGIE WATTS: It is, because women are very intimidated.

JIM GAFFIGAN: Stand-up is a strange life, so it makes traditional or "normal" dating virtually impossible.

FRED ARMISEN: [laughs] Oh my god.

JENA FRIEDMAN: What's the "oh my god" about?

FRED ARMISEN: Is it hard to date?! Um, is it hard to date, since I've started doing stand-up? It's the same.

BOB ODENKIRK: [pauses, then laughs loudly] Well, I've been married for twenty-four years, so, uh—

JON STEWART: I'm stunned. Are these real questions?

JENA FRIEDMAN: Yes.

JON STEWART: [laughs] It was the only way I could date, sadly. . . . I love that their concern for a female comic is, "You went into comedy, are you prepared to die alone?"

JENA FRIEDMAN: It's a real concern!

JON STEWART: [driving] By the way, I just let someone go even though I had the right of way, and I don't know if you can capture that type of altruism [in the interview]. . . .

JENA FRIEDMAN: For sure!

JON STEWART: And I'm not even sure I got a wave on it, but that's fine.

Do you write your own material?

FRED ARMISEN: [pause] Yes!

PATTON OSWALT: I really do! I guess it's a compliment when people tell me, "You could totally hang with the lady comics!"

REGGIE WATTS: [laughs] Oh my god. Uh. Yes. Most of it. Actually, it writes itself.

JENA FRIEDMAN: Why did that make you laugh?

REGGIE WATTS: It's just like the most, like, I guess backhanded. It's just so, come on, man, Jesus Christ. "Well, we gotta prove women are just as funny as guys are, so just to be sure, do you write your own material? We're hoping it's yes." I mean, what the fuck, come on!

JIM GAFFIGAN: Yes. Well, occasionally I write with my wife.

JON STEWART: [laughs] I have a team, almost like a construction crew.

EUGENE MIRMAN: Um. Sorry, another call was coming in. I wasn't stumped by the question [laughs]. The real answer is: yes. I'm trying to think of a joke answer—

JENA FRIEDMAN: This is the one question people get the most offended by.

EUGENE MIRMAN: Oh, I'm not offended!

JENA FRIEDMAN: Oh, I know, I know! [laughs]

EUGENE MIRMAN: I just wanted to be like "a penguin writes my material," but I wanted it to be a better thing than that [laughs]. I'll say that I write my own material, but in a week I might email you with a better joke.

JENA FRIEDMAN: You can totally do that!

EUGENE MIRMAN: Right, right.

JENA FRIEDMAN: I just wanna make you guys feel safe, not like how I was when I was asked these questions.

EUGENE MIRMAN: [laughs] When you did all these interviews that are on record. Yes, I think the correct answer is I write my own material.

BOB ODENKIRK: [pause] YES! No one else is to blame for how bad my material is, just me.

JENA FRIEDMAN: Have you ever been asked that?

BOB ODENKIRK: No, never been asked that. It's ridiculous. Nobody should be asked that after 1972.

Is all your material about being a dad?

JIM GAFFIGAN: No.

JON STEWART: That's a tough one, because you could see that not being viewed through the lens of pure sexism but somebody who actually knew the act and could be like, "Are you just having children to get another fifteen minutes?"

JENA FRIEDMAN: [laughing] I feel bad for whoever I asked that question to via email and not via phone call, like Jim Gaffigan, because his interview was via email and I think I offended him!

JON STEWART: Aw, man, that's funny.

BOB ODENKIRK: [laughing] No, just very little of it.

EUGENE MIRMAN: Um, if I hope to take my comedy to the next level, I will stop doing stand-up about weird things that have happened to me and I will switch mostly to fatherhood. My comedy is a mix of what happens to me, which now incorporates fatherhood.

FRED ARMISEN: None of my material is about being a dad. I'm not a dad.

JENA FRIEDMAN: I'm sorry, I just assumed since you're a man that you're a dad.

FRED ARMISEN: No.

Do you do any material that isn't about your gender?

JIM GAFFIGAN: Yes.

FRED ARMISEN: [laughs] Often, yes. I do a lot of material that isn't about my gender. I might even say that I don't think any material is about my gender.

REGGIE WATTS: Uh, yeah. I do a lot of stuff that isn't about my gender. I think the only way to help equalize the equation is to really move away from calling out the obvious. That's how I look at it.

JENA FRIEDMAN: Do you think I'm calling out the obvious?

REGGIE WATTS: [laughs] No! Well I think you gotta call out what you're feeling! But it's why I never do material about being Black. I mean, you can see me.

JON STEWART: [laughs] Well, in this patriarchal society, in essence, no I don't, because the foundation of all my material is the authority that I wield.

JENA FRIEDMAN: Wow.

What's it like to work for Jon Stewart?

JON STEWART: Tedious.

Are you easily offended?

REGGIE WATTS: No.

JIM GAFFIGAN: I like to think I'm not easily offended.

FRED ARMISEN: No, I am not easily offended.

JON STEWART: [pause] They asked that to a comic?

JENA FRIEDMAN: Yeah.

JON STEWART: Just a question, "Are you easily offended?"

JENA FRIEDMAN: Yeah.

JON STEWART: [Pause] Yup.

JENA FRIEDMAN: [laughs] You're the only one who answered yes!

JON STEWART: I am easily offended.

JENA FRIEDMAN: Thank you for being an ally.

JON STEWART: I am easily offended. By the way, if you're in comedy, you're easily offended, just by different things. The whole point of comedy is we take offense to things. Of course we're easily offended. That's the craziness about PC culture, we can't complain about people giving shit to you about something because our entire careers are based on giving people shit about things, we just think it's the right shit.

JENA FRIEDMAN: That's so vulnerable. No one else wanted to admit that they could be offended. That's such a feminist gesture.

JON STEWART: Aw, thank you.

What's it like to be away from your kids?

JIM GAFFIGAN: It's hard. I joke around [about] it being a relief, but it's actually very difficult.

BOB ODENKIRK: It sucks, it's terrible. It's the hardest part about being in show business for me and a source of great sadness through a chunk of my life.

Do you have help?

REGGIE WATTS: No, not really.

FRED ARMISEN: Yes. Collaborators, writers. Yes.

JENA FRIEDMAN: I mean in terms of domestic help.

FRED ARMISEN: I have a handyman who comes around once in a while. I have a housekeeper who comes every week, and gardeners . . . so that would count as domestic help.

Who takes care of your kids when you're working?

JIM GAFFIGAN: My wife.

BOB ODENKIRK: My wife does. I've certainly done my share when she's working, too.

JENA FRIEDMAN: It's so funny, because the last time I heard your voice was during the Howard Stern interview and it was so good and nuanced and I'm just reading off a list of questions female comedians have gotten and I feel like such an asshole. Thank you for being my guinea pig, because these are so uncomfortable to ask.

BOB ODENKIRK: No, I love it. This is a smart idea. You've got a good idea here. Keep going.

JENA FRIEDMAN: Um, all right [laughs nervously] . . .

Do you think women should accept Louis C.K.'s apology?

BOB ODENKIRK: Do I think women—am I trying to tell women how I think they should feel? It's a tough one, but there's no question that his situation is a complicated one, but in my mind, I would hope that people would accept his apology over time, because I think he's genuine in it. Part of the process we are going through, there has to be some place for forgiveness in the world.

FRED ARMISEN: I make no generalizations. I think every individual has their own personal reaction and decision to make about that.

JIM GAFFIGAN: Well, I can't speak for an entire gender or even another individual's viewpoint on the matter.

EUGENE MIRMAN: [laughing] Whatever each person feels like is what they should do.

REGGIE WATTS: [deep breath] No.

Do you think men should accept Louis's apology?

JON STEWART: [laughs loudly] For which offense?! [laughs] That's funny.

What was your personal experience with Louis C.K.?

JON STEWART: More jokes, less penis.

EUGENE MIRMAN: He would do shows at a Chinese

restaurant when I lived in the Somerville area twenty-five years ago, when he would record Dr. Katz. So he would come and do sets.

REGGIE WATTS: My experience is that he's very much all for himself at the cost of others' well-being.

What's your work/life balance?

PATTON OSWALT: I'm very lucky in that my wife is very supportive and tries her best to cover the "dad" role when I'm gone. Plus, she's very understanding, and is so good with the sort of "switching the roles" of me out being the breadwinner.

JIM GAFFIGAN: It's ever-changing. There is no week or month that is the same.

BOB ODENKIRK: 99 percent work, 1 percent life. I'm a modern man [laughing].

REGGIE WATTS: Well, you know, it's okay. I have to worry about a lot of things, I really fight for my right to be paid less for the same amount of work that I do compared to women, but I enjoy it.

FRED ARMISEN: I feel like work is part of my everyday life. It's mixed in. It's not a split thing. It's all kind of the same.

EUGENE MIRMAN: Normally it's more life and slightly less work. More just taking care of my son during a pandemic, and stand-up is currently a dangerous art form.

JON STEWART: I don't have one and I've never been asked to have one.

But back to Louis . . .

JON STEWART: [laughs] That is a segue worthy of Matt
Lauer.*
REGGIE WATTS: Yes, finally.
EUGENE MIRMAN: [laughs] Go on.

**I'm interested to know what degree you think his comedy
has changed, and what degree you think the way we have
experienced his comedy has changed.**

EUGENE MIRMAN: I think with the news that came out, it
affected people's perception of his likability. . . . I do love
how many questions you get about Louis. It's really funny.
JIM GAFFIGAN: I haven't seen any of his comedy in years.
REGGIE WATTS: Oh boy. I don't think his comedy has
changed at all. I think that we all think that he's kind of a
douchebag.
JON STEWART: Wow. Wow. [pause] That's just, who asked
that—
JENA FRIEDMAN: Isaac Chotiner from the *New Yorker*. In his
defense, he did give me a heads-up that he wanted to talk
about Louis.

---

* Jon went on *The Today Show* in 2017 to promote an autism benefit, and in the
middle of a story about a child having a breakthrough, Matt Lauer interrupted
to ask him to comment on Louis.

Were you at *Late Show with David Letterman* when the controversy occurred with him sleeping with female employees?

JIM GAFFIGAN: I appeared on his show a couple times during that period, but it never came up. I don't know why it would.

FRED ARMISEN: No, I wasn't. [pause] What the fuck? What is that? It's so distant! The whole thing is so distant. "Were you in Norway when that serial killer killed all those people on that little island?" No.

EUGENE MIRMAN: No, I've never worked on a late-night show—wait, were you there?

JENA FRIEDMAN: No, but I did work at *Letterman*, so that is a question that is in the bounds of acceptable.

EUGENE MIRMAN: Meaning that's a question that you got? But you worked at *Letterman* for some period?

JENA FRIEDMAN: Yes, it is, and I did work at *Letterman* for a year. And the thing with the intern happened before I was there, and it wasn't a bad question because it probably did influence me never really meeting him. I just thought it would be funny to ask that question to someone else.

EUGENE MIRMAN: Right, right.

JON STEWART: [laughs] I might have been. I was a guest pretty frequently. I may have been there during that time.

There's Amy Schumer and Lena Dunham, who are outspoken feminists, but who also raise concern about "white feminism." Is that a concern for you as well?

REGGIE WATTS: White feminism? Uh, is that a concern for me as well . . . uh, I . . . you know, I really don't think about it [laughing].

FRED ARMISEN: It's not . . . It's such an impossible question. It's also unfair to Amy and Lena. How is a person supposed to answer that?

JENA FRIEDMAN: Exactly [laughs].

Your fellow comedians like to joke about how you slept your way to fame. How accurate is that criticism?*

JON STEWART: [laughing] Oh my god! So many suppositions in there that are just brutal! I will say this, for men that would be posed as tongue-in-cheek for the ludicrousness that that could be a question.

Tell me a joke.

JIM GAFFIGAN: I'd rather not.

EUGENE MIRMAN: That's fair, uh, that's a question that interviewers don't ask me but that I get in general in

---

* Andrew Goldman, "There Is No Escaping Whitney Cummings," *New York Times*, September 16, 2011.

regular life that always feels unpleasant, because stand-up is the illusion of a conversation, not a real conversation, so I don't have a jokey joke.

JENA FRIEDMAN: That's a good answer. I think non-comics don't realize what a weird question it is.

EUGENE MIRMAN: Maybe ask Mel Brooks and what he writes in, you can use as my answer.

JENA FRIEDMAN: That's a good joke!

BOB ODENKIRK: My DVR is completely full of shows about hoarders.

JENA FRIEDMAN: I am sweating asking these questions.

BOB ODENKIRK: I don't mind telling you a joke, but I don't want to tell a reporter a joke [laughs].

JENA FRIEDMAN: Oh, for sure. I told him that's the comedian's equivalent of "show me your tits."

BOB ODENKIRK: Yes. That's right. It's true! Well, that is your joke. Jena, that's the best!

JENA FRIEDMAN: We get these questions all the time, so we become—we're in offensive mode.

BOB ODENKIRK: It's easy for me to answer it as a novelty. The difference is, when you're asked that question, you're asked to assume so many assumptions ingrained in it that are ridiculous and fucking insane and you don't get to laugh at them. You almost can't answer the question. If I answer your question, then I am accepting your presuppositions, which are insane and yet come across, are culturally . . . I mean, do you write your own material is such a weird thing to ask someone after 1972 and the fact that a modern female comic might be asked that is insane.

JENA FRIEDMAN: I love that you're answering these questions with a sincerity that I wasn't prepared for, and I really appreciate it.

BOB ODENKIRK: Of course.

FRED ARMISEN: [pause]

JENA FRIEDMAN: Fred, tell me a joke?

FRED ARMISEN: [long pause] Um, this is like a form of performance art where my joke is just this silence and these few words, so it's a sort of an abstract joke.

JENA FRIEDMAN: That was funny. Did your girlfriend write it?

FRED ARMISEN: [laughs] No, I came up with it on the spot.

Do you have any jokes before you go?

JON STEWART: [laughs hysterically] That's mind-boggling.

Have you ever been asked any of these questions?

PATTON OSWALT: I have never been asked anything even REMOTELY like these questions. The fuck is wrong with people?

EUGENE MIRMAN: No. I'm often asked when was I interested in doing comedy. But nobody would ever say "man in comedy." I think that the way they are phrased, it's really that gender is being shoehorned into stuff that feels wildly unrelated to the act of comedy. If I go through interviews, I am asked a lot of strange stuff, it's not just gender-y.

JIM GAFFIGAN: No. I've received many "lazy" questions from reporters, such as "describe your comedy" or "Do you only do food jokes?" but nothing as flatly insulting as these.

JON STEWART: There were a couple that I have gotten like, "Tell me a joke." And the question about work/life balance, but based on them knowing I spend too much time in the office.

REGGIE WATTS: No. Maybe one about being a minority, but not really.

How did it feel to be asked them?

REGGIE WATTS: Tiresome.

JON STEWART: Demoralizing.

JIM GAFFIGAN: It was strange. I think it provides insight to the perspective of how female comedians are viewed by entertainment writers and society at large.

BOB ODENKIRK: It's hard to hear these questions and go, "Who would have asked these questions? That's insane." But the truth is, a lot of people would ask this and they see the world this way . . . there's a lot to make fun of in the world still.

EUGENE MIRMAN: To do an interview that has all these questions that are not about you feels odd. Can someone be attractive and funny? The answer is obviously yes, it's at the edge of a question. . . . The irony is, people think they are doing something unique but they are doing the opposite.

FRED ARMISEN: I felt like there was something removed from the whole thing. Me as a comedian, this has nothing to do with anything I have ever done. You could be talking to some stranger about any job. I felt like "This person isn't even interested in comedy." It's like a child asking a question, a child who doesn't understand how the world works. "At a hospital, do you have appointments?" It's shocking, it's so funny.

JENA FRIEDMAN: Thank you for being so brave. [laughing] And I'm sorry if any of the questions—

JON STEWART: You don't need to be apologetic for any of it. Exposing what's considered best practices in journalism when it comes to comedians who are women, you don't need to apologize for putting a light on that.

JENA FRIEDMAN: Thank you.

JON STEWART: The other thing is that you're not hurting us to get to that point, at all. We're in the business of saying things, and if some of the things we say get pushback, the truth is, all the things we say at some level get that and that's just the business we're in. I feel your struggle with wanting to make sure everyone is safe. But, Jena, you can't.

JENA FRIEDMAN: I just want to make men feel safe [laughs].

JON STEWART: [laughs] By the way, it doesn't go unnoticed—[laughing] but do you know what I mean? I just hear it in your voice, you're doing a smart and funny thing and you're doing it well and you don't need to apologize for that.

Canceled Comedians Say

the Darndest Things*

It's always kind of funny when a famous comedian whines about cancel culture on a platform where we all can hear them. Whether it's Bill Burr in an *SNL* monologue or Dave Chappelle in one of his many Netflix specials,† getting paid millions to speak freely about being unable to speak freely is the ultimate flex . . . and I want in on it, too!

By writing about cancel culture in this book, I hope to insert myself into the subgenre of comedians paid to complain about cancel culture (see, some women really can have it all!). Only I don't take issue with cancel culture itself, just with the idea that it's anything new.

In comedy, the looming threat of being canceled has always

---

*Including myself, if this essay doesn't do it for you.
† I'm gonna get so much shit for this.

169

come with the territory. In 1927 Mae West was charged with obscenity (i.e., canceled by the government) and sentenced to ten days in prison.* Between 1961 and 1964, Lenny Bruce was arrested multiple times on obscenity charges and after an eight-month-long trial, he was eventually convicted.† In 1972 George Carlin was arrested for performing his "Seven Words You Can Never Say on Television" routine at SummerStage in Milwaukee.‡ A judge later dismissed Carlin's case, and no boundary-pushing American comedian has been arrested for their words (or performed in Milwaukee) ever since!

And the practice of canceling is as old as time; maybe it predates time. Socrates was put to death for teaching his students to question the status quo. Jesus was crucified (but not by the Jews) for espousing a politically destabilizing philosophy that threatened Roman rule. Joan of Arc was burned at the stake for "cross-dressing, heresy, and witchcraft" (aka just being a teenager). Who's to say there wasn't some disgruntled Neanderthal man in the Maltravieso cave who got canceled for scribbling over prehistoric art with a drawing of his dick? Who knows what went down before we had a historical record (or Instagram) to document everything?

But what's different now is the addition of social media. (Plus the twenty-four-hour news cycle, clickbait journalism, coordinated digital disinformation campaigns in the form of troll farms and targeted fake news, and algorithms that amplify our outrage to

---

* Patrick Bunyan, *All Around the Town: Amazing Manhattan Facts and Curiosities* (New York: Fordham University Press,1999), 317.

† Douglas Linder, "The Trials of Lenny Bruce," Famous Trials, 2003, www .famous-trials.com/lennybruce/566-home.

‡ Jim Stingl, "Carlin's Naughty Words Still Ring in Officer's Ears," *Milwaukee Journal Sentinel*, September 29, 2007.

keep us online.) These are the phenomena at the heart of why nuanced, empathetic discourse has become virtually impossible, why some old-school comedians are mad as hell, and why this thing we call "cancel culture" is thriving.

So what is cancel culture anyway? For starters, it's hard to define, and I think that's what makes discussions around it so pervasive. If this neologism didn't encompass such a wide array of ideas and meanings (is it mob rule, public shaming, online bullying, or vigilante justice?), people wouldn't constantly be arguing about it.

And because the term is so nebulous and elicits so much emotion, any issue you can bend to fit into its bucket makes great fodder for journalists, pundits, politicians, and comedians to weigh in on, and more importantly, profit from.

Fox News host, mascot of white privilege, and possible 2028 Republican presidential candidate* Tucker Carlson rarely has anything substantive to say, and yet somehow he still has so much airtime to fill. He relies on tropes like cancel culture to stoke racial grievances and keep his conservative white viewers enraged and engaged. For example, in the aftermath of the January 6, 2021, attack on the US Capitol building by right-wing extremists and a few random grandmas, most news outlets were blanketed with coverage and analysis of things like white supremacy, homegrown terrorism, details about the Capitol rioters and the elected officials who aided them.† However, during that same period, Fucker‡ Carlson focused on a story about six racist Dr. Seuss books being

---

* Yeah, I know, you should be scared!

† The best evidence we have that Trump orchestrated the January 6 attempted coup is that it didn't succeed.

‡ It's a typo, I swear!

phased out of print by Seuss's *own estate* as "evidence" of cancel culture.

And it's not just the right wing: late-night comedy's favorite alleged John,* Bill Maher, railed against cancel culture that same month. During his tirade—I mean monologue—Maher brought up the story of Emmanuel Cafferty, a worker who was fired after being falsely accused on social media of being a white supremacist. While the incident is an egregious example of public shaming, the real culprit in Cafferty's case wasn't cancel culture but rather the lack of workplace protections, which enabled his employers to fire him at will and without due process.

Don't get me wrong,† internet-era abuses such as online shaming of private citizens and targeted harassment (like doxxing) are dangerous and damaging. When they're cited as examples of cancel culture, they make the phenomenon almost impossible to defend.

But I don't think stopping bullying is what truly motivates men like Tucker Carlson and Bill Maher to continually rant about cancel culture, mostly because both of those guys seem to love bullying. (Carlson has repeatedly berated individual female journalists on his program, while Maher's bullying is a little less pointed and typically reserved for people who are overweight or who follow Islam . . . or both!)

I think oftentimes what's really behind powerful people's fear of cancel culture is a fear of accountability. In an era of increased transparency, if you're a celebrity and you profit off your trusted persona and then you violate that trust by saying or doing some-

---

* https://www.thedailybeast.com/bill-maher-shames-sex-workers-after-onlyfans -reversal.

† "Don't Get Me Wrong" would have made a great tagline for any comic who came up in the 1980s.

thing stupid, you may get called out for it, you may even suffer some negative consequences. This sort of comeuppance is relatively new. For so many famous men who have made their name and a shit ton of money being arbiters of politics, culture, and public sentiment, it's suddenly uncomfortable to realize how the tables have turned.

The #MeToo movement was a prime example of a mass, mainstream effort to hold abusers accountable. Since so few perpetrators of sexual misconduct and violence are ever prosecuted, the court of public opinion is often victims' only hope at retribution. During the movement, our collective consciousness shifted (maybe for the first time in HIStory) toward believing victims. Bad actors (and good actors like Kevin Spacey) were finally named and shamed, and in a few egregious cases, investigated, prosecuted, and imprisoned (and then in most cases, released from prison). This new culture of accountability filled in the gaps where the criminal justice system failed.

Yet just a few years later, many of the people (men and women, well, one woman) "taken down" in the #MeToo movement, particularly the comedians, are still working, winning Grammys, or in the process of staging their comebacks (Cosby 2024!).

And on a side note, if you're a female comedian and you're ever offered a well-paid gig touring with a "Me Too" (our cute nickname for workplace safety hazards credibly accused of misconduct), I will never hold it against you for taking it. A job is a job, and if you're strapped for cash and need the money, no judgment here. Just be safe out there and tell Louis I say hi!

Which brings me to another point about cancel culture: a lot of the time, it barely makes a ripple. In most cases, when the punishment doesn't fit the crime, the fallout is often short-lived. Emma Grey Ellis in *Wired* magazine notes, "People who are canceled usually don't stay that way, and often the attention just fuels their success. Many of the canceled people whom the *New York Times* name-checked last year are no longer canceled—Taylor Swift, *Queer Eye*'s Antoni Porowski, and Chris Evans seem to be doing fine. Nearly everyone, even people canceled for things that are actual crimes, is still working, still has fans, and, you know, is a millionaire."

That said, there are always exceptions. I can think of at least one example where someone tweeted something stupid and it fucked up their entire career, because I WATCHED IT UNFOLD IN REAL TIME on my first day as a staff writer for the second season of the *Roseanne* reboot.

I just want to preface: I didn't submit for the job. But apparently, Roseanne had seen my stand-up on *Conan* and her producers reached out to my reps to gauge my interest in writing for the show. Would I be interested in joining the writing staff of one of the most-watched TV shows in America as our country was literally slipping into fascism? I couldn't say no.

Sure, it wasn't a perfect fit. I had no prior experience writing on a network sitcom or for a QAnon supporter. But maybe it would be an opportunity to help bridge the cultural divide? If I wasn't able to write for Roseanne, I figured I would at least be able to write around her, for characters like Darlene and Jackie, and to push story lines that challenged the views of a critical mass of Americans who seemed happy with the direction our country was going (or, more accurately, falling).

Growing up, I loved Roseanne, the frank, feminist working-class heroine. So what if Roseanne 2.0 was a right-wing nut? I wasn't. Maybe it would be good for my point of view to be echoed in that writer's room ... after all, *if you're not at the table, you're on the menu*, at least that's what I told myself when I apprehensively accepted the job.

Right after I was hired, I started following Roseanne on Twitter to get a sense of her voice . . . and what a voice it was! As I scrolled through her conspiratorial tweets, I couldn't believe she still had a show on a family-friendly network. Her micro-blog musings were so insane they even inspired me to delete my whole Twitter feed.*

A few weeks later, when I read that racist dog whistle about Valerie Jarrett, I was literally sitting in the back of an Uber (I'm still not comfortable driving in L.A.), heading onto the CBS Radford lot, about to embark upon my first day of work.

"Oh fuck," I thought as I read all the justifiably outraged responses to Roseanne's tweet. My eyes remained glued to social media as I walked into the building and watched my new job opportunity evaporate as quickly as it had appeared. When I finally looked up from my phone, I noticed that my office was situated next to the office of one of my comedy heroes, Wanda Sykes. I reassured myself that if Wanda didn't have a problem with Roseanne's tweet, then I guess I shouldn't, either? Just then, I looked back down at my phone to see that Wanda did have a problem with the tweet. In fact, she was quitting over it. Damn it. Should I quit in solidarity now, too? Was I complicit or profiting off white supremacy if I stayed? About an hour later, the decision was made for me. *Roseanne* the show and Roseanne the comedian had been canceled.

When ABC canceled *Roseanne*, I wasn't surprised. Even though I was physically sick to my stomach to be out of such a lucrative and intriguing writing gig, it was refreshing to see that in Trump's

---

*I don't believe I have any content on Twitter that would get me into trouble, but in any event, I do delete my feed from time to time. It's like a digital colonic.

America a person could still be held accountable for their racism. I just wish it had been him.

I feel bad for Roseanne and for how it all went down. I don't believe that in that moment her intent was racist as much as it was a thoughtless tweet from a famous person with mental health issues who should never have been on social media. But as a white woman, it's also not my place to weigh in. It doesn't matter if someone is consciously or subconsciously racist. If they put those views into the world, it can still cause damage. Words matter, and if you are lucky enough to be in a position of power where your words are seen and heard, you should wield that power responsibly or risk losing it.

• • •

Something often overlooked in conversations about cancel culture is how gender and race factor into who gets canceled and why. At least in comedy, it seems as if female comedians are often held to account for their words more than many male comedians are for their actions (and by actions, I mean sex offenses).*

We saw it in the manufactured outrage to Sam Bee calling Ivanka the one c-word in America slightly more offensive than Clinton and in the bipartisan blowback to Michelle Wolf's 2018 White House Correspondents' Dinner speech (watch Elayne Boosler's 1993 speech for context; it was just as edgy, but with shoulder pads). Kathy Griffin was put on a terrorist watch list and lost tons of work for posing with a replica of Trump's severed head (which I, too, felt was harsh, but only because of how it was

---

* Gilbert Gottfried getting fired as the voice of the Aflac duck for an insensitive tweet is one exception.

lit). While Kathy is STILL paying the political price for that photo (Anderson Cooper and CNN, can you please invite Kathy back on your New Year's Eve countdown already?), Kathy's collaborator, the photographer Tyler Shields, suffered no major consequences for his role in the image/PR debacle.[*]

Women of color in comedy have it even worse. They have to navigate so many minefields just to be in a position to succeed in the white, male-dominated entertainment landscape. If they do get canceled, it's often for something even more benign than a misguided tweet or an edgy photo shoot. Oscar-winning icon Mo'Nique was blacklisted just for asking for equal pay. Comedian Dina Hashem got death threats for an off-color joke she wrote and performed on Comedy Central about a slain rapper. Comedy Central ended up caving to public pressure and pulled the comic's entire set off the internet. If Dina had been a white guy telling that same joke and not a Muslim female, one can only imagine how different the public's response or the network's reaction would have been.

But even as I cite examples of the double standard, there are always counter-examples to prove me wrong. For instance, there's Shane Gillis, a male comedian (it's fun to write "male comedian" as if it's not inherently implied) who was hired by *SNL* for being a comic who appealed to conservatives[†] and then got fired a week later for pretty much the same thing (assuming appealing to conservatives includes spewing racist slurs on a podcast). Does his case refute my point that it's most often women who are held accountable for our words? Maybe? Or maybe Shane as an ideologi-

---

[*] It might even mark the first time in recorded history that a man didn't take credit for his work.

[†] Lauren Bradley, "SNL Cast Shane Gillis' Conservative Appeal," *Vanity Fair*, September 2019.

cal affirmative-action hiring cancels out his canceling . . . got that? I'm still trying to wrap my head around it, too. I don't have all the answers; no one does. That's why this topic is such a dizzying one.

But after all is said and said, there is one thing that makes me doubt that this phenomenon we call cancel culture really is the blight on free speech and democratic society that so many of its critics claim it to be. And it's that I'm not afraid of cancel culture, whereas I, dear reader, am afraid of EVERYTHING!*

As a political comedian† in the line of fire, I should be paralyzed in fear at the thought of a McCarthy-era brigade of PC mobs coming for my career, but I'm not, because they're not. Sure, I've been harassed online (pretty intensely and quite a few times by people all over the political spectrum, as well as by trolls and bots) and suspended from Twitter (only once, but it was worth it).‡ I also have outdated content online that I'm not exactly proud of, but I'm also not afraid of being canceled over it.

Famous comedians who've had their own jokes called into question on social media for being transphobic, homophobic,

---

*Things I'm afraid of include but are not limited to: infectious diseases, asteroids, earthquakes, tsunamis, catastrophic climate change, wildfires, car accidents, driving in Los Angeles, serial killers, hypodermic needles on the beach, skin cancer, all other types of cancer, exploding potholes, STDs, meth heads, Guinea worm, brain-eating amoebas, contaminated water, plane crashes, fascism, communism, Nazis, guns, mass shootings, terrorist attacks, crowds, dying alone, dying in a group, dying young, fucking up this book, fear itself.

† And a writer, director, multi-hyphenate, nano-influencer, and actor with very little range.

‡ I was suspended from Twitter for eighteen hours after tweeting that Stephen Miller, Mike Pence, and Donald Trump had contracted Covid four months before they actually did, just because they were running around without masks on at the height of the pandemic and I knew their contracting Covid was inevitable, so I decided to tweet fake breaking news about it in advance. To this day, it remains a crowning achievement.

misogynistic, etc. are often the same comics who blame audiences for being overly sensitive or who equate cancel culture with censorship. Few consider the alternative: maybe the joke in question is not funny.

In *American Cunt*, I wrote a few jokes about Caitlin Jenner and the openly trans MMA fighter Fallon Fox in a segment about gender that in retrospect aren't that funny. Since Caitlin had just come out as a Republican and Fallon had only started fighting women after she transitioned, I thought the jokes about them were fair game. Later, when I saw my five-minute segment reposted on a TERF (trans-exclusionary radical feminist) YouTube channel, I was mortified.

The original bit that I had constructed to fit within an hour show about gender and politics now looked like some anti-trans diatribe, which was the opposite of my intent. When I scrolled through the transphobic comments praising the set, I finally understood how my jokes in a different context could be perceived as dangerous. When you see people weaponizing your words to discriminate against a vulnerable population, words you may have thought were just harmless jokes suddenly don't feel so funny.

At the time, no "woke" Twitter mob came for me demanding that I apologize, but if they had, I would have readily apologized. I was sorry. I still am. I had no interest in defending those jokes, and I tried my best to reverse the damage. I publicly denounced the YouTube channel on Twitter, deleted those jokes from my show, and rereleased the album without them.*

---

*To any comedians reading this who blame cancel culture when audiences react negatively to your jokes, at least take comfort in the fact that audiences are listening.

Of course, established comedians who came of age before the internet might have a harder time acclimating to this brave new world of social media, where everyone now has a microphone and anyone with even a remote platform is always one tweet away from getting fired.

None of this dismisses the validity of cancel culture, which I believe is mostly a by-product of the growing pains we're experiencing at the intersection of cultural evolution and social media. I also think conversations about cancel culture, as annoying as they may be, are necessary to our growth as a society—they should just happen off-line, in less emotionally charged spaces, where people can actually see each other's faces and recognize each other's humanity.

It would be great if people online exercised more compassion and restraint before rushing to judgments or harassing others, but that's never going to happen as long as we have an unregulated, anonymous internet that profits off our collective outrage.

It would also be great if people in power could stop being such creeps and assholes, or if workplaces and the criminal justice system could hold people who commit sexual misconduct accountable so that the internet doesn't have to, but that, too, is never going to happen.

And finally, it would be great if the famous comedians who make so much money whining about cancel culture could just look inward and evolve (it's not that hard, guys), but that's never going to happen, either, because at the end of the day, they're not really being canceled.

Stand Down

Recently I had an epiphany: in my fifteen years working as a stand-up comic, I've never once been invited to tour with a headlining male comedian. When I was coming up in comedy, male comics (aka comics) almost never invited female comics on the road with them, for obvious reasons (bringing a female comic on the road makes it harder to cheat on your spouse). If a male headliner did invite a woman to open for him,* it was often because he was sleeping with her or at least angling to. Even the many cool, kind male comics who weren't opportunists or predators didn't often take female comics on the road with them, perhaps because it could still create the wrong impression.

I think back to a conversation I had with some younger female comedians who informed me that an acquaintance of mine, a "woke" headlining male comic, had been inviting younger, unwitting female comics on the road with him and then propositioning

---

* Please excuse the double entendre, which is way too on the nose.

them. When I heard this, I was infuriated. Why was this shit still happening? What made it even worse was that this comic was a self-proclaimed "ally" and he should have known better. I didn't want to confront him directly, partly because the female comics had told me their stories in confidence and I didn't want to betray their trust, but also because he wasn't an anomaly and he wasn't technically doing anything out of bounds. There is no unwritten rule among headliners not to hit on their opening acts, and even in a post-#MeToo era, my acquaintance's predatory behavior, sadly, wasn't that uncommon. But it should have been, and there should be a rule among people in power in every industry not to prey on people who work for them. As a headlining comic myself, I thought maybe I could get the ball rolling on that, and where better to do it than on the comedian's equivalent of the office water cooler, Twitter?

> Hey, headlining comics, if you take a younger comic on the road with you, don't try to fuck them . . . comedy clubs are work environments. Extend an employment opportunity to that younger comic but don't be creepy about it. Also, if you are, they will probably tell us. We all talk.

It was a pretty innocuous tweet, or so I thought, and I forgot about it as soon as I pressed send. But apparently, the tweet resonated and circulated among comedians and somehow got on the radar of a famous male comic, who ranted about it on his podcast the next day. Even though the comedian never mentioned my name in his rant, his fans soon found out that I was the female comic who had authored the apparently triggering tweet. Later, a blogger from the website Chortle transcribed the famous comic's rant:

[REDACTED COMEDIAN] reacted to the comment on his podcast, saying: "Some fucking female comic says 'hey headliners . . . ,' gave us all a stern talking-to, 'whether you're innocent or not' . . . why don't you go talk about your twat for another hour onstage? You fucking hack. Jesus fucking Christ! My God."

Offering his impression of Friedman's act, he went on, "Then I stuck my other finger in it . . . for an hour!" before imagining the outraged reception he'd receive. "Don't say she's a dirty comic! Her body, her jokes! Oh my God!"

After a few threatening messages from random men online, I followed with a little Twitter rant of my own, where I tried to bait the famous comic into responding to me (I can be a troll, too) . . .

In comedy, there's no HR department, so people who care about equitable work environments have to put pressure on people in power to care too . . . @REDACTEDMALECOMEDIAN, if you disagree, feel free to tell me to my face.

I'm not trying to police anyone's consensual behavior, but in a work context, maybe we should let the person who isn't in power dictate the terms of the dynamic? Ideally, there should never be an expectation for sex in a work environment that isn't sex work.

I realized it might not be the best use of my time to poke a hornet's nest of angry comedy bros, and so I gave up and deleted all my tweets on the subject. Sometimes, having an opinion on the internet, even if it's the correct one, can be more trouble than it's worth.

What bothered me most wasn't the way this critically and commercially successful comedian mischaracterized my act (nothing against vagina jokes, but I don't really have any), but that he's a powerful, influential person in my industry and an employer. Imagine if a CEO at any company with an HR department had reacted in a similar way?

I don't know how to make the world safer other than by calling out bullshit when I see it, even if it pisses off some powerful people. At least after fifteen years, I'm finally at a place in my own career where I have the luxury to do that, but it took a while.

As a young comic, I knew enough not to say anything when a reputable festival booker overseeing a talent showcase took a drunk colleague from that showcase up to his room after the show or when a cable channel exec sent a friend Louboutins and asked her out on a date after she had just pitched a project to him that she was trying to get sold. I was auditioning to be in that festival, too, and getting paid to work with that channel. And even if I had wanted to support my friends and blow the whistle on this creepy but totally normalized behavior, how would I have done it? Talk to the festival's founder, who allegedly was just as creepy? Reach out to the cable channel's management, who were all good friends with that executive?

In an unregulated industry like comedy, it's always been left to individuals to protect themselves. Coming up, I was keenly aware of this. I was always so careful—maybe sometimes too careful. I rarely ever went out drinking with the guy comics after our shows, which made it even harder for me to ingratiate myself into the male-dominated scene. But it was only because I knew I was operating in a sexist and sexually charged work environment and I wanted to be taken seriously and succeed on my own terms.

Early on, I witnessed a few female colleagues fall into the inevitable trap of sleeping with male comics and then suffering professional consequences after those relationships soured. And although "shitting where you eat" didn't always go badly, it wasn't a gamble I wanted to take. In my twenties, whenever a more established male comic or booker (aka a potential mentor or employer) would take an interest in me, I'd often wonder, "Is he being cool because he likes my comedy or because he wants to sleep with me?"* About half the time, it was the latter, which was still enough to make it hard for me to trust any of them. If I felt that a comic I wanted to work with was interested in me romantically, the next question I'd ask myself would be, "How do I 'friend-zone' this guy without him resenting me or retaliating by talking shit about me to other people or icing me out of work opportunities?" Both of which have happened. It was exhausting trying to navigate these tenuous "work" relationships, hoping not to offend or alienate anyone while also trying to pay rent and build a career.

Ultimately, I branched out from stand-up and into writing, producing, and directing, partly because after five years of performing, I still wasn't able to make a living off the income I was generating from my club gigs alone (to be fair, most comics don't). I watched some of my favorite female stand-up comedians who came up before me struggling to break through, and I quickly realized that I had to find another job that was stand-up adjacent if I wanted to remain in comedy. Fortunately, I was lucky enough to

---

* Or both!

get a comedy writing job, and then another one, and then another one as I continued to perform stand-up on the side.

I also feel so thankful that I have been able to pivot to writing, producing, and directing comedy, because I have a lot more control now than I ever did when I was slugging it out in the clubs. I hated having to rely on other comedians, bookers, and industry gatekeepers, many of whom seemed either consciously or subconsciously sexist (and sometimes, the female gatekeepers were even worse).

I hadn't thought about how frustrating that time in my life was until I listened to that universally beloved, multimillionaire comic rage against my dumb tweet on his podcast and was reminded why I moved away from stand-up to begin with. But the good news is it's changing. Now, more than ever, more women and other marginalized people are achieving success in mainstream comedy. A lot of that has to do with social media leveling the playing field, people speaking out and demanding equity, and the old-guard gatekeepers becoming obsolete.

Up until recently, I had never gone on tour with a famous female comic, either,* mostly because there have always been so few of them, but also because historically, female comics have been discouraged from bringing lesser-known female comics on the road with them (there can only be one at a time, ladies!). So when the opportunity arose, I didn't know what to expect.

To my surprise and delight, it was a blast. It was inspiring to be a fly on the wall of her tour, to see up close how she engaged with her crazed fans as well as how she adeptly and respectfully man-

---

*I had opened for female friends, but most of us barely make enough money on tour to pay our supporting acts a living wage.

aged her robust team of agents, managers, producers, comedians, and assistants, who all seemed excited to be there, working for her. The experience was also a little bittersweet; if only I had had this opportunity a decade earlier when I really needed it. At this point in my life, I'm not sure that's my goal anymore—but it was pretty cool to see how it can be done.

One of the Good Ones

The first headlining comic I ever opened for was Jeff Garlin. I was living in Chicago, and I had just performed on a holiday show for *HEEB* magazine, a short-lived, edgy, Jewish hipster publication in the mid-aughts. Jeff was visiting from Los Angeles, and he stopped by our postshow dinner to say hi to some mutual friends. At one point during the dinner, Jeff mentioned to the group that he was performing the following night at Zanies, a comedy club in Old Town, and that he was nervous about it because he hadn't done stand-up in a few months and he was a little rusty. I didn't know Jeff, but I did have a few drinks and I thought it was kind of silly that a famous comic would be so nervous about performing on his own live show (this was before people had cameras on their phones). So as he mulled over his preshow anxiety, I deadpanned, "Whatever you do, just don't let me down." A few people at the table chuckled. Jeff looked at me, smiled, and said, "Why don't you open for me?"

"Seriously?" Surely he must have been joking, but he wasn't.

"I don't have an opening act yet," he said matter-of-factly. I sobered up.

"But you've never even seen me perform. How do you know I'm funny?" I should have just shut up and taken the gig, but I really did think he was messing with me. I had worked so hard for the past two years to get any stage time whatsoever, and I had never imagined it could be this easy. He explained his logic.

"You were on the show tonight and it sounded like it went great. Plus, I'm looking for an opener for tomorrow's show and I can tell you're funny. It's a talent of mine."

And that was that. I was opening for Jeff.

The next night, I proved him right. I did ten minutes on his sold-out Sunday night show at Zanies and I crushed it. After my set, I floated into the greenroom, high on adrenaline. Dave Pasquesi, a brilliant actor and improv hero of mine, was there along with some other veterans of the Chicago scene, who were also friends with Jeff. Dave had watched my set. He shook my hand and complimented my performance. I was over the moon. One of the best feelings in the world is discovering that someone you so deeply admire appreciates your work. In the weeks that followed, now that I had Jeff Garlin's endorsement, I started working more at Zanies, one of the few comedy clubs on the North Side of Chicago that actually paid.*

Jeff and I stayed in touch, and a year later, after I moved to New York, he was headlining Carolines on Broadway and he invited me to open for him again. I had another great set (his crowds were

---

*From my personal experience, the comedy clubs on the South Side of Chicago, which were predominantly Black owned and operated, paid comics far more than many of the predominantly white, North Side comedy rooms.

always cool), and at that show, I met my first comedy manager. This manager also worked with Jeff and was later instrumental in getting me a meeting (this was after a junior manager at that same management company had fired me) that, along with my writing packet, would help me land my first real comedy job, writing for *Late Show with David Letterman.*

Jeff once told me that to succeed in show business, everyone needs someone else to reach out their hand and lift them up. His words comforted me—to think that someone so successful was once just another young, struggling comic in need of help gave me hope. It's intuitive when you think about it, but I felt so helpless when I was first starting out and looking for mentorship or any guidance anywhere I could find it. I didn't know how to go from performing at open mics to getting booked spots, to getting paid gigs, to getting a manager and an agent, etc., and there were no comedy podcasts back then to guide me. I had to rely on word of mouth among my peers or anyone else I met along the way willing to impart any nuggets of wisdom on how to succeed in this unconventional business, like the comedy manager who once told me to "just do it." I'm sure he was just reading off the bottom of his Nike shoe, but to this day it remains the most salient advice I've ever gotten from a comedy manager.

I was lucky to meet a few people early on who later became friends and mentors. But there were a lot of men (and definitely some women, including two female executives at a cable channel who seemed to go out of their way not to book female comics*) who weren't so kind and who made it so difficult for me, and so

---

*From 2008 to 2011, of the eighty-eight comics given comedy specials on that channel, only ten were women.

many of my female peers, to succeed. As my brilliant friend, comedian Eliza Skinner, so perfectly summed it up to me, "We were swimming in a toilet."

When Bob Saget passed away in 2022, dozens of comics took to social media to mourn his loss and sing his praises. Jen Kirkman, a hilarious comic who I sometimes get mistaken for, just because we're both feminist comedians with similar-sounding names, reflected on a brief encounter she'd had with Bob after a bad set she had at an outdoor daytime festival (I don't think anyone can have a good set at an outdoor daytime festival, but that's beside the point). Jen was feeling down, and Bob, who was at the festival as well and had seen her set, went out of his way to give her a pep talk. In a tweet, Jen praised Bob and lamented, "I am deeply saddened that there are so many creeps in comedy that when one of the non-creeps talks to me, I can't fully enjoy it, accept it, or trust him due to what the creeps have done."

When the #MeToo movement* started bubbling up in the wake of an admitted sex offender's presidential inauguration, it felt like abusers in power might finally get their due. But like all social movements, it was flawed (it's over now, so I can speak about it in the past tense). For a brief moment, the movement shifted public consciousness and inspired so many conversations about what constitutes sexual harassment and assault (versus what's considered a "bad date" with a famous person who literally wrote the book on dating), but it also didn't really bring about much meaningful social change.

It also barely scratched the surface on all the creepy or subtly sexist behavior that doesn't fit neatly into the definition of assault

---

* Shout-out to activist Tarana Burke, who started the movement.

or workplace harassment—particularly in industries that don't have conventional workplaces—but that can be just as damaging.

The more insidious abuses of power that aren't technically prosecutable offenses or HR violations (assuming your job has an HR department) are so endemic, so persistent and universal, that they make it so much harder for disenfranchised people in every industry to succeed.

When I started working in comedy, I was low-key preyed upon so often by random men in positions of power in my industry: so many of my female colleagues were as well. The toxicity led some of my female friends to stop pursuing comedy altogether, partly because of what a pernicious work environment it was. In my personal experience, many of the less obvious forms of harassment often left me feeling worse than the groping, ass-slapping, and more overt stuff. To this day, I don't even know what to call those encounters: are they "micro-harassments," "macro-annoyances" (don't make fun of me, I'm just spitballing here), or just an unfortunate but inevitable by-product of working in any unregulated industry, specifically one that relies on cultivating relationships (oftentimes with more powerful men) to achieve success?

I remember the first time I thought I was close to getting my stand-up on TV, a rite of passage for any touring comedian. A reputable booker had emailed me to see if I wanted to get lunch and talk about a tape that I had sent him. I assumed he was interested in working with me because I had met him in a work context and he seemed to like my stand-up. I had been doing comedy for about three years by that point, so I was still somewhat green, but I was so hungry and hardworking and I was so excited to get lunch with him. I believed—or naively hoped—that maybe this respected booker saw my potential and might be interested in helping me get my stand-up to the next level. During our lunch, instead of talking about comedy, he shifted the conversation to our personal lives. He told me that he was single and asked me a series of intimate questions about my own dating life. I tried to bring the conversation back to comedy, but I got the vibe pretty quickly that he wasn't interested in talking shop or in working with me. I ended the lunch early and never did get that audition. What he did (maybe) wasn't technically harassment, but it also wasn't cool. I don't believe he's a bad guy, and he is no longer in that job, but I do sometimes wonder how many dreams he and people like him squelched along the way.

Then there was that time I got a little too drunk at a festival overseas (I was hazed by the locals!), and a headlining comic who was twice my age (and also sober at the time) invited me to get food with him after our show. Since all the restaurants were closed by the time our show ended, he suggested we order room service in his hotel room. I had spent the previous two days hanging out with that comic. I trusted him and I thought we had become friends, so I took him up on his offer. Before the food even got to his room, he started kissing me. I let him. I was drunk and young and alone in a foreign country. When he suggested we get naked, I politely declined and got the hell out of there. Was it dumb of me to go to his hotel room in the first place? Absolutely. Did I ever feel unsafe? Thankfully, no. I was lucky that he wasn't a "bad guy" (the bar is low), but later, when I made it clear that I didn't want to be involved romantically, he ended our brief friendship and never really spoke to me again. I didn't even care about what transpired in that hotel room. The aftermath—his callous behavior and dismissal of me as a person, all just because I didn't want to sleep with him—that genuinely bothered me, and still does to this day.

On another occasion, I was sitting at the comics' table at a comedy club when a famous male comedian took an interest in talking to me. Was it a privilege that he focused on me over the other young comics vying for his attention at the table? Sure. Did my male peers resent me for it? Yep, and they later gave me shit for it, too! In the next few months, that older, successful, veteran comic would frequently message me on social media to tell me how cute he thought I looked in certain photos. I would deflect his flirty comments with self-deprecating jokes or just ignore them. I was also lucky by then to have a whisper network of female comedian friends, who informed me that this guy slept with a lot of younger female comics and to be wary of his intentions. I was a fan of his work and I wanted him to like me, but I didn't want to sleep with him. A few weeks later, he emailed me and asked me out on a coffee date. I countered by asking if I could shadow him on the set of a television show he was directing at the time. It was a bold move on my part, but I wanted him to get the message that I didn't want to date him. I wanted to be a director and I was looking for a mentor.* He never responded. Years later, the other young guy comics at that table would go on to open for him, whereas I would never hear from him again.

Then there were the countless other times when I wasn't actively preyed upon for being a young, heterosexual, anonymous female in comedy, but I also wasn't taken as seriously or treated the same as many of my male peers. These incidents are even harder to identify, because implicit biases like sexism and racism are everywhere and factor into so many scenarios, particularly in an

---

*Maybe the secret to getting a guy harassing you at work to leave you alone is to ask him to be your mentor?

industry that is so subjective. I'll never forget this one time I interviewed for a great writing job. I had already sent in two packets, so the producers liked my jokes, and now they wanted to meet me to see if I was "the right fit" for the show, whatever that meant. Selling myself in a room had never been a problem for me. I once even talked my way into a highly competitive management consulting job I had zero qualifications for. Part of why I got the client-facing job was probably on account of my privilege. As a young, sociable female in a white-collar industry under pressure to diversify, I stood out from the applicant pool of mostly nerdy male engineers.*

When I interviewed for this comedy-writing job, I was comforted by the fact that the person interviewing me was also a comedian, whom I had recently met at a show. The night we met got kind of crazy and devolved into a bunch of comedians at a bar being subjected to an incredibly raunchy after-hours drag show, where the main act pulled all sorts of random objects out of his ass and flung them into the crowd. It was definitely an interesting night, but nights like that weren't all too uncommon in New York's downtown performance-art scene in the mid-2000s. Now, during my interview, all of a sudden his tone shifted to sound more serious.

"You know this job isn't going to be fun," he said. I laughed, imagining he must have a warped view of what I considered fun.

"It's a job. I'm not expecting it to be fun," I joked. I referenced my résumé, which included college internships in banking and tech and eighty-hour workweeks at a stiff health-care consulting firm in Chicago. I reiterated that I had no expectations for this job to be fun, and I thought it was a little odd that he felt like I needed

---

*I was also a good bullshitter, which constituted 90 percent of the job requirement.

the disclaimer. The rest of the interview went well, but afterward I stewed over it. Why did he think I needed the job to be fun? What did he mean by fun? It was a WGA writing job and it paid roughly $4,000 a week, including health insurance. Regardless of how "not fun" it was, it would have been an incredible opportunity for me, or anyone. I wondered if this employer cautioned prospective male hires about how not fun the job was as well. I wondered if I had fucked myself over right from the start by meeting him in a social, somewhat raunchy context to begin with. Either way, I didn't end up getting the job. Was it because he only saw me as a party girl and didn't think I was serious enough to work in a room full of professional comedy writers? Or maybe because there was a better candidate? I'll never know, but I'll always wonder.

I don't want to come across as if I think every interaction is predatory, or any job I don't get is because of my gender (when, in fact, a lot of writing jobs I do get in majority-male writers' rooms are partly because of my gender), but I do know that as frustrating as it was for me to navigate all these encounters as a young, college-educated white woman, I can only imagine how much worse it must be for so many other people who are less empowered, people who work in low-wage industries with little to no job protections, undocumented people, or people who have kids to support or dependents to care for, or all of the above.

The positive legacy of #MeToo is that it reaffirmed how much power we can derive from sharing our stories. The more we all talk about the vast spectrum of abusive behavior and injustice so many women and marginalized people endure, the closer we can get to defining it, understanding it, and hopefully diminishing it.

I'd like to think we'll get there someday. I've seen so many improvements in my fifteen years in comedy, and in so many workplaces in America, it's better for women and marginalized people today than it has ever been. And while we're waiting for our employers and people in power to evolve, at least we've been emboldened by our increasingly loud whisper networks and by a culture that seems to want positive change.

The irony here is that this story begins with a glowing anecdote about my onetime employer and mentor Jeff Garlin, but most recently he's become known for leaving his job on a successful sitcom, *The Goldbergs,* after an HR investigation into on-set verbal misconduct. I don't know the details of that investigation, and I'm not questioning them. I can only speak from my own experience, back then a young comic with no credits to my name, when Jeff was always kind and respectful to me. I will always be grateful to him for how helpful and avuncular he was to me when no one else was looking, and when I needed it most.

It is kind of funny and does put things into perspective: the comedian taken down for accusations of verbal workplace misconduct (according to the *Hollywood Reporter*), is someone—when compared to so many other comedians, bookers, industry execs, and gatekeepers I've encountered along the way—I always considered to be one of the good ones.

Maybe there are no good ones? Or maybe what it means to be good changes over time or according to our own lived experiences? There is no great unifying theory as to what to do about the everyday biases and misdeeds that are so rampant and pervasive in every industry. But I do know this: if you help out the people under you, treat them with respect, and expect nothing in return, who knows, maybe someday when you could use a little positive PR, they'll write something nice about you in their first book.

Oh, the People You'll Meet!

've encountered quite a few creeps and weirdos in comedy over the years, but I've also actively sought some out, like the now-deceased cybersecurity entrepreneur and alleged murderer John McAfee (RIP John) or the infamous "Cannibal Cop" Gil Valle, an NYPD police officer who spent time in prison for plotting to eat women online. Few things bring me more joy than trolling eccentric public figures and revealing a less sound-bite-ready side of pop culture's rogues' gallery that mainstream media outlets often ignore.

For as long as I can remember, I wanted to be a *Daily Show* correspondent. When the want became an intent, I still had no idea how to submit for the job. So I started interviewing eccentric characters on my own and posting those videos on YouTube, in hopes that a producer or a casting agent might see my work and ask me to audition. That never exactly worked out, but the segments that I self-produced did actually help me land a job working behind the scenes at *The Daily Show*, producing segments for other correspondents.

The first self-produced interview I ever conducted was with the affable and quirky single-issue NYC mayoral candidate Jimmy McMillan (aka the Rent Is Too Damn High Guy). Jimmy was a lovely and charming, if somewhat incoherent, interview subject. He was also surprisingly easy to get in touch with (I found his contact information on his website and emailed him directly). A few days later we met in an office building in midtown with a camera crew I had cobbled together through my network of comedian friends.

I had never conducted an interview before, so I was quite nervous. I started off by asking some softball questions about his policies, but I pivoted when I realized he didn't have any answers other than "the rent is too damn high." Our conversation on his candidacy somehow evolved into a meditation on love and relationships.

The end result was an oddly humorous, offbeat interview that lives on YouTube to this day. A year later, that awkward interview got the attention of *Daily Show* producers, who asked me to consider a field producer role at the show. Initially, I passed on it. I was a performer and writer and didn't see myself working in production. Comedian Wyatt Cenac, who I had met through stand-up and who was a correspondent on the show, encouraged me to keep an open mind. Wyatt said the job was actually more writing and directing than producing, and that it would teach me how to be a filmmaker, and he was right. I ended up working as a field producer at *The Daily Show* for the next three years. It was basically film school.

As much as I liked giving my jokes away to any correspondents who would take them, after two years behind the scenes, I really wanted to be on camera. Maybe I needed to make another video where I would be on camera to beef up my portfolio? But with whom? I thought about it as I strolled around my neighborhood. It would have to be someone funny, and recognizable, and someone I'd actually be able to convince to sit down with me. I realized the answer was staring me in the face, literally. I would interview the man whose picture was on every mailbox and lamppost in a ten-block radius of my apartment: Dan Perino.

Dan was a bit of a local celebrity in Lower Manhattan, known for the thousands of flyers he plastered around the city that read LOOKING FOR A GIRLFRIEND. If you're unfamiliar with this hyperlocal nano-celebrity, his flyers said it all.

> *I'm really looking for a girlfriend. This is not a joke. . . .*
> *I am a professional artist and creative person. You*
> *know who you are. To me each and every person is*
> *beautiful. Open to the possibility of the relationship*
> *morphing into something more profound.*

I was single myself, and while Dan wasn't really my type, I empathized with his plight. I googled him to see if any other outlets had covered this hopeless romantic's quest for love and was floored by all the media attention he had gotten. In an interview with *Vice*, Dan came across as far less sincere and a lot sleazier than I had imagined he'd be. When *Vice* reporter Jules Suzdaltsev asked about Dan's dating criteria, the canvasser Casanova responded:

She's gotta be smokin' hot. No old ladies, gotta be 25 to 30s. No 40-year-olds. . . . If I'm doing a movie, or if I'm doing this documentary, she'll be there right by my side. So the public won't·see a fugly woman around my arm. I don't fuckin' want that, a fugly woman. Keep 'em away from me. I want the damn models.

Right then, I knew I had to interview Dan, if for no other reason than to warn any unsuspecting women who might be tricked into dating him. I contacted Dan to see if he'd be down to meet up on camera, and he immediately responded yes. On the day of the shoot, just as I was leaving my apartment, I spotted an HIV test I had lying around (don't ask). I thought it might make for potentially interesting content, so I brought it along.

It was edgy, but Dan had bragged in local media about having unprotected sex with multiple women since the start of his campaign, so an STD test seemed fair game. To my surprise, Dan was totally into it. He took the rapid test on camera as we waited awkwardly for the results. The tense small talk during those twenty minutes was hilarious:

"You should be a reporter," Dan said, as if he somehow knew I wasn't one.

"Thank you."

"You're far better than some of these interviews that I've had."

"Thank you."

"You have a hell of a personality, which goes a long way with me."

"Oh."

"And if it were under different circumstances—"

"Like me not giving you an AIDS test?" I said as I tried not to laugh.

"I would definitely ask you out."

Dan was a good sport throughout as I teased him mercilessly, and the rest of the interview went great. The other day, a friend texted me a photo of Dan's flyer on an East Village street sign. Apparently, eight years later and through a global pandemic, he's still at it!

So many things I've worked on have led to other, weirder jobs.

My silly interview with Dan made the rounds among New York online media folks and caught the attention of Jen Carlson, the deputy editor at Gothamist, who reached out to see if I wanted to write an essay for Gothamist about my reactions to the hit Netflix true-crime show *Making a Murderer* (which I watched and live-tweeted in one weekend).

Since essay writing is my Achilles' heel (I can't believe we've made it this far, dear reader!), I asked Jen if we could produce a video instead. We kicked around some ideas for the segment and landed on me potentially interviewing Ken Kratz, the prosecutor in the case, who was never interviewed in the *Making a Murderer* docuseries because he had refused to sit down with the filmmakers.

I really wanted to interview Ken—he seemed like such a . . . character—and I was prepared to finance the production myself. It was a tall order, attempting to track down this elusive guy, but as luck would have it, Ken was heading to New York to shoot a piece with *Dateline NBC* that week anyway, and somehow we convinced him to let us interview him on that same trip. I was ecstatic. My filmmaker friend Jake Salyers and I assembled the crew as Jen finalized details with Ken.

But on that cold January day in 2016 we were scheduled to shoot, Ken was radio silent. By six p.m. that evening, Jen had reached out to Ken multiple times, but we still hadn't heard from him. I was finishing up at work when Jen called, unsure of what to do.

"Tell the crew to start setting up. I'll head over soon and we'll figure it out," I advised her, even though I had no idea what to do, either. When I got to the Gothamist offices in Dumbo, the whole crew had set up and Ken was still nowhere to be found. Was he bailing on us? There was only one way to know for sure. I would call Ken myself, from my own phone (there are burner apps you can use now instead, which I highly recommend), and beg him to come if I had to. To my surprise, Ken answered.

"Hello?"

"Hi, Ken. This is Jena Friedman. I just wanted to see what time you're coming by."

"I had a long day shooting. I'm heading back to my hotel at the Waldorf Astoria," he said. Damn it. Our fears were confirmed: Ken was out. I blurted out the first thing that came to mind.

"The Waldorf Astoria has bedbugs. I can't believe they put you up there. Tell the car to turn around and take you to our offices in Dumbo. I promise, it'll be fun . . . and less itchy," I ad-libbed. It was now close to eight p.m. and dark outside. I knew the chances of Ken traveling to Brooklyn to film a segment with an unknown interviewer for an unknown website were slim.

Don't judge me for what I am going to tell you next—I had one more producer trick up my sleeve and I wasn't afraid to use it. During my research on Ken, I had gotten the vibe that he was a bit of a creeper from some stuff I had read about him on online message boards, including accusations that he had sent unwanted sexts to a domestic violence survivor involved in one of his cases. I really wanted to call him out on that, too, but I would need to get him to sit down with me first. Since I've always believed the end justifies the means (within reason), I asked Jen to take a picture of me, smiling coyly and seated across from an empty chair with all our lighting set up.

I typed: *We're such fans, and we all can't wait to meet you!* under the photo and texted it to Ken. I'm not proud—I mean, I'm so proud that as a last resort, I thought to use my waning looks to trap an alleged sexual predator into my comedy web.

But would it work?

To our shock and horrified glee, it did! Ken actually showed up. For just under an hour in a warehouse in Dumbo, I channeled my best impression of an actual reporter and probed (maybe not the best word) Ken with all sorts of questions related to the case.

"There are a lot of conspiracy theories around this case." I said. "I'm going to say a name, and you just tell why they didn't do it."

"Let me tell you first of all why I'm unwilling to do this. First of all it's unfair to the people you're about to name—"

"I was going to name Netflix."

The end result was priceless. Ken showed a side of himself that was as icky as it was amusing, and I got to score an interview with someone who even Netflix couldn't wrangle. After the interview, Ken stayed in touch, only because he had my cell phone number. After a series of texts, I stopped hearing from him because I blocked him.

The interview with Ken Kratz, along with some other comedic videos I had made and posted on YouTube, apparently got on the radar of Adult Swim, and a year later in 2017, I found myself working with the comedy network to develop a special of my own.

Part of why I landed on this edgy comedy channel's radar was because media outlets had recently called out Adult Swim for gender bias* and after a PR debacle, the network was now apparently working to bring in more women—I guess that meant me?

When I met with Adult Swim's creative director and founder,

---

*According to journalist Megh Wright, out of forty-seven shows on Adult Swim's 2016 slate, ZERO were created by women. Megh Wright, "47 Men, 0 Women: Why Doesn't Adult Swim Order Shows from Female Creators?" Vulture, June 14, 2016, https://www.vulture.com/2016/06/47-men-0-women-why-doesnt-adult-swim-order-shows-from-female-creators.html.

Mike Lazzo, for lunch in Atlanta to talk about developing a project with his network, one of the first things he did was apologize for public comments he had made, and then retracted, justifying his network's gender blind spots.

I didn't need an apology. After all, I wasn't one of the many female content creators that Adult Swim overlooked, like the insanely hilarious sketch group Variety SHAC (with Shonali Bhowmik, Heather Lawless, Andrea Rosen, and Chelsea Peretti), who got as far as making a pilot for Adult Swim, but the network never aired it. Furthermore, I had been so consumed with the 2016 election outcome that the Adult Swim drama was barely on my radar.

And then Mike shifted the conversation: "I've been reading your tweets, and you seem angry."

"That's an astute observation." I laughed. "I'm shocked that you wanted to meet."

I didn't give a fuck.

Mike Lazzo was in the media doghouse, Trump had just become president, and I was over pretending to be cool with the casual sexism that was (and still is) everywhere, even if it made me seem "angry" to a potential employer. Mike then told me that he had watched a bunch of my clips online and that he loved the series I'd written, codirected with the director Keola Racela, and produced, parodying the *New York Times* wedding videos.

He asked if I would be interested in making a scripted series for Adult Swim based off that premise, which was about a serial killer and his oblivious bride planning their wedding. I loved that project, and turning it into a TV show had always been a dream of mine. But in this new era, I had more pressing concerns.

"What do you wanna do?" Mike asked.

I thought about it and responded, "I wanna make your demographic not hate us."

Mike smirked. I wasn't joking.

In the naive pre-Trump years, some of the content on Adult Swim, including one overtly misogynistic and racist "alt-right" sketch show I won't name here, might have been dismissed as ironic or subversive. Most mainstream media critics didn't see it for what it was: a gateway to more extreme hateful views. If I was going to work with a network that perhaps inadvertently amplified views of the alt-right, I wanted to produce content that had the polar opposite message. Content that could potentially educate male viewers to be better—but in a way that was actually funny (it had to be funny) and not like a TED Talk or a PBS after-school special.

Enter *Soft Focus*.

To Mike Lazzo's credit, once I signed on to work with Adult Swim, he was supportive in every way. He paired me with incredibly talented producers from *The Eric Andre Show* and gave us a generous production budget (by Adult Swim standards) to ensure that we would be able to actualize our vision. Our network executive, Matt Harrigan, who first showed my comedy to his colleagues at Adult Swim, was instrumental in our show's success and gave great notes along the way that only added to the comedy (a rarity in TV and one thing that makes working with Adult Swim so cool).

We shot more segments than what would ultimately air, like an epic desk interview with fired CNN pundit Jeffrey Lord and a cold open with a set piece of a twenty-foot-tall vagina (the joke being that network execs had commissioned the "feminine" set, since they were so excited to have a "female presence" on the channel), but in the end, what we landed on was really unique and hilarious.

Each episode began with a comedic field piece in the vein of *60 Minutes* or *Nathan for You* but about feminist issues (like campus rape, sexual harassment in gaming, anti-trans bathroom bills, and one segment we never got to make about revenge porn). To close out the show, and to reward our audience for watching the first act, I would end each episode by interviewing a creep.

The first creep I interviewed was Gil Valle, aka "Cannibal Cop." To this day, people always ask me if I think he would have actually eaten his wife if he hadn't gotten caught. After studying up on him and reading his autobiography (okay, I listened to it on tape during my walks home from the production office), my conclusion is a resounding YES (don't quote me). His wife was so suspicious of him that she put spyware on his computer and alerted the FBI herself. You don't go to those lengths unless you're afraid of being eaten. If I found out that my husband (hi, Josh!) was plotting online to eat women, I wouldn't think much of it, because I know him and know that he'd never actually go through with it (he's a picky eater and also not a cannibal). Ask yourself right now: if your partner plotted online to eat people, would you alert the authorities? Probably not, UNLESS YOU FELT YOU HAD REASON TO BELIEVE YOUR PARTNER WOULD ACTUALLY DO IT. That seemed to be the case with Gil.

By the time I met Gil, he had been so dragged through the court of public opinion, it seemed like he had nothing left to lose, which is also a dream disposition for someone you're about to interview. Nothing that I could say or do would bring him more shame than what he had already endured, and our interview (and the subsequent dating game we sprang on him) proved just that. Gil was a great sport and seemed to genuinely enjoy our serious interview morphing into a dating game. We were also very careful to keep the contestants far away from Gil throughout the whole production—not that he would have done anything, but he wasn't the first creep to be on a dating game,* and in the unlikely scenario that any flesh eating were to happen, I didn't want blood on my hands.

For the second installment of *Soft Focus*, I interviewed John McAfee,† the infamous cybersecurity entrepreneur who had fled Belize in 2012 on allegations of murder. I was wary of putting a spotlight on an alleged rapist and murderer, but John was planning to run for president as a Libertarian candidate in 2020, so I felt that he, too, was fair game. Plus, if 2016 taught us anything, it's to take even the most absurd presidential candidates seriously.

On the morning of the interview, my skeleton crew and I drove to John's compound in an undisclosed location (I guess now that he's dead I can tell you: it was on the Outer Banks of North Carolina). I was apprehensive about meeting John, not just because of the allegations against him, but because we were meeting him at his compound and no one on my team knew what to expect. In hindsight, I do not know how we got insured to do that piece in the first place (I credit our executive producer, Josh Cohen, for pulling that off). When we showed up, any reservations I had about the interview were confirmed and amplified by the presence of John's five heavily armed guards, who were all carrying semiautomatic weapons as they patted down our crew.

---

* Serial killer Rodney Alcala appeared on *The Dating Game* in 1978, and he won! Women love bad boys ☺.

† In June 2021, John died by suicide in a prison in Spain, where he was being held for tax evasion. Or did he? I know there are some conspiracy theories around his death, since he had faked his death once before, but I have no doubt that John took his own life—it's the most Libertarian way to go.

At first John was dismissive of me. Before the cameras started rolling, whenever I would ask him a question to break the ice, he would respond to my male producer instead of to me. But as I started to tease him and as he started to drink more whiskey, he warmed up to me. After talking with him for a few hours, I found him to be charming and charismatic but equally batshit insane. In fact, none of my questions seemed to faze him:

"If you could murder someone—else, who would it be and why?"

"The entire leadership of the Sinaloa cartel," he said without flinching.

The interview went perfectly, meaning that no one on my crew got shot (although at one point I did come close). In the end, we got enough usable footage to make a great segment. That night the other producers, Josh Cohen and Griffin Pocock, and the crew and I celebrated our coup by jumping into the Atlantic Ocean.

The *New York Times* described *Soft Focus* as "a gonzo feminist perspective . . . that doesn't just crack jokes about misogynist violence. It offers the giddy pleasure of payback," and the *Guardian* called it "thrillingly unexpected: a bold blend of feminist politics and heart-in-your-mouth edginess." Yet despite widespread critical acclaim, *Soft Focus* sadly never went to series. The irony is that the network's controversial founder, who had been quoted as saying "women don't tend to like conflict," became our show's biggest champion, and a year later when he stepped down in 2019, the prospect of *Soft Focus* going to series disappeared with him.

But it was fun while it lasted.

A year later the *Soft Focus* interviews, as well as a stand-up performance on *Conan*, where I poked fun at our nation's true-crime industrial complex, would help land me my next gig: my first (and so far only) television series. Here's an excerpt from that *Conan* set:

Women don't watch true crime—we study it to make sure we don't end up on it. And true crime is kind of feminist. It's the only time the entertainment industry will take a chance on an unknown female lead....

How would I know that making fun of true crime would land me a true-crime show of my own? But it did, and I felt weird about it. When executives at AMC reached out to gauge my interest in making a "somewhat funny, feminist true-crime show," I honestly didn't think it would be possible. Then the pandemic happened, I lost six months of tour gigs, and I realized, anything's possible!

When I met with producers and started to envision what the show would be, I knew I wanted to do things differently than most other true-crime shows—no crime-scene photos of dead people, no interviews with serial killers, no overly drawn-out narratives just to keep people engaged . . . etc. I felt a responsibility to the victims and their families not to tell their stories in vain and to use our platform to raise awareness about the less sexy systemic injustices (misogyny, racism, homophobia) that are so widespread but also so often ignored.

I was still unsure whether comedy and true crime could coexist in the same show until we shot the pilot episode, where I interviewed Dr. Martin Blinder—who stands out as maybe the worst person I've ever interviewed. Dr. Blinder was the defense's expert witness in a case involving Steven Steinberg, who stabbed his wife Elana to death while she lay sleeping in her bed in Scottsdale, Arizona, in 1981. At trial, Blinder somehow convinced the jury that Elana's "constant nagging" drove her husband to kill her. I know. And what's worse is that it worked. Partly because of Blinder's "expert" testimony, Steve was found "innocent by reason of insanity" (a defense that was abolished in Arizona, thanks to this case), and the jury acquitted him.

But the Steinberg case isn't the only case in which Dr. Martin Blinder's "expert" testimony swayed a jury. He's most well known for the "Twinkie defense," where he testified that Dan White, the guy who shot and killed San Francisco city supervisor Harvey Milk and San Francisco mayor George Moscone in 1978, was "not of sound mind" during the double political assassination because, according to Blinder, Dan had eaten too much junk food in the weeks leading up to the trial and the sugar impaired his judgment.

The more I researched Blinder, the more I learned about his reputation for delivering pseudo-scientific, victim-blaming defenses for a paycheck. I also learned that he had been married twice before and that both his ex-wives had apparently killed themselves (in deaths that remain suspicious to this day). You can't make this shit up.

I was shocked when my producer informed me that Blinder was game for the interview (apparently, he didn't google me in advance). I hadn't interviewed anyone or even performed in almost a year, so I was a little rusty. Furthermore, I had never interviewed anyone who I had such a strong negative reaction to (not even Cannibal Cop!), and I wasn't sure I'd be able to keep my cool. Everything I'd read about Blinder, including on his own website, repulsed me, and during our Covid-safe* interview, it was hard to mask my complete disdain for him.

I wasn't sure how the segment would turn out until I got into the edit bay and realized I had captured on camera what I couldn't

---

*While I normally wouldn't have exposed an unvaccinated octogenarian to my antics during a pandemic, Dr. Martin Blinder was an exception.

put into words: his abject misogyny. One of the most jaw-dropping moments from the interview happened when I asked Blinder how he was able to diagnose Steven's psychotic break from the brief time he spent with the defendant. The interaction (condensed for clarity) went as follows:

DR. MARTIN BLINDER: I began to see aspects of this woman [according to an hour or so interview with her killer] whose very perfection must have been maddening . . . sex was limited to two minutes on Saturday afternoon. That was the extent of their sexual contact.

JENA FRIEDMAN: Every Saturday?

DR. MARTIN BLINDER: I don't know what the calendar was.

JENA FRIEDMAN: Was the two minutes her fault?

DR. MARTIN BLINDER: Well, she went down on him for two minutes, because she didn't enjoy sexual intercourse anymore.

JENA FRIEDMAN: Because it was two minutes?

DR. MARTIN BLINDER: If you're a forty-year-old man and you haven't had sex in a week, two minutes is a measure of endurance. . . .

It's hard to articulate what it felt like in that moment as I listened to this somehow established expert in his field justify his blatantly sexist testimony from four decades earlier. It felt like I had been transported back in time, or into an episode of *Mad Men*. I wondered how any jury could ever have taken him seriously, but they did, for decades.

Ultimately, the Blinder interview was one of the most cathartic interviews I've ever done. Here was a guy who flew under the radar for so long and caused so much pain, revealing his true nature during our brief, on-camera conversation. I believe his deeply ingrained sexism is what caused him to underestimate me as well, and what compelled him to let his guard down and reveal his true nature to me on camera. It's also such an indictment of our society that this charlatan was able to evade public scrutiny for so long.

While I'll never be able to undo the damage Blinder wrought on the families of the victims he slandered, it felt good to expose him for the fraudster that he was and to raise awareness of how the expert witness industry works, and how it has the potential to subvert justice.

Toward the end of my interview with Blinder, I asked the doctor about his own biases. Flustered, he responded:

DR. MARTIN BLINDER: You're crafting your questions in a
    construct that misleads.
[A light bulb went off, so to speak . . .]
JENA FRIEDMAN: I'm almost like an expert witness.

Blinder grew silent, for the first time since I'd sat down with him. I knew right then that this tricky, genre-bending show we were developing might actually work. I had done the impossible: I had beaten the bloviating expert narcissist at his own game.

A few months later, our comedic true-crime series was green-lit. I guess I have Dr. Blinder to thank for that.

The Night Before Covid

probably shouldn't have taken the gig.

Ever since I was a kid, I've been terrified of infectious diseases to the point of near paralysis. In fact, after I saw the 1995 thriller *Outbreak*, I developed a sort of OCD tic where I would check under my bed every night to make sure a spider monkey wasn't hiding out there, waiting to bite me. Were there any spider monkeys in the Philadelphia suburb of Haddonfield, New Jersey? No. Even if there had been, would they have been able to find a way into my bedroom and hide out there undetected? Probably not. Yet that didn't stop me from being a neurotic little weirdo for longer than I feel comfortable admitting here (I think I continued to check under my bed for hypothetical disease vectors well into my teens). For the next two decades, I would keep tabs on any infectious disease outbreak around the world in a way that's not too dissimilar to how I imagine sports fans keep up with their favorite teams (only I wouldn't be rooting for the virus).

So when news of a novel coronavirus in Wuhan, China, first

appeared on social media in early January 2020, I was already pretty freaked out. By February, it seemed inevitable that the world was about to shut down, but very few people in my orbit seemed to register that, or if people were actually concerned, many just jokingly shrugged it off. I was supposed to go on tour in a few weeks and I was wary of traveling. When I called my touring agent to ask whether I should cancel my upcoming six-country tour, she informed me that none of the venues were canceling shows and that if we pulled out prematurely, we might be liable for any production costs. Great. That said, she understood how apprehensive I was and she assured me that she'd support my decision to do whatever made me feel comfortable (retreat to a bunker in a sparsely populated wooded area?).

I weighed my options. It was pretty clear that live comedy would be fucked for quite a while and that my impending tour might inevitably not happen. But I had this one gig coming up in Upstate New York, and I needed to make money before I would lose my ability to make any money touring again in the foreseeable future. It was scheduled for February 7, and the flights that I had already purchased to get there were nonrefundable.

I phoned my infectious-disease doctor friend Dr. Amesh Adalja, whom I had first met when I cold-called him in 2014, under the guise of "researching a field piece for *The Daily Show* on the Ebola outbreak in West Africa." The truth is, there was no such field piece. I was just losing my mind and hours of sleep every night as I tuned in to BBC reports on how quickly Ebola was spreading in West Africa. At the time, very few US media outlets were reporting on it, and I wanted answers.

"Do you think Ebola will mutate and become airborne?" I whispered, not wanting my colleagues, who knew I wasn't working on an Ebola-inspired field piece, to overhear. Dr. Adalja, a senior scholar at the Johns Hopkins Center for Health Security, matter-of-factly responded, "It doesn't need to mutate and become airborne, because it's already doing such a good job killing as is." Right then, I knew we'd be fast friends.

On a side note, I was so obsessed with Ebola in those months that at one point during work, Jon actually stopped by my desk and kindly asked me to "take it down a notch" with all my Ebola hysteria (I had already sent in a few pitches on the subject that week). He assured me that the outbreak seemed to be under control and that it wasn't something we needed to worry about. The next day, a Liberian citizen who had recently flown into Texas from a hot zone became the first person on US soil to be diagnosed with the virus (RIP, Thomas Eric Duncan). Suddenly I wasn't so crazy after all! Cut to Jon, on the show that night, wearing a cartoonish yellow hazmat-suit costume as he performed a segment the show's writers titled "Au Bon Panic," about his fears of a potential Ebola outbreak on US soil. I finally felt seen.

My Ebola obsession reached its peak a few days later, when some random guy actually recognized me while I was waiting in line to pick up food at B&H Dairy.

"Are you obsessed with Ebola?" he asked. I wondered what gave it away. He continued, "You're Jena Friedman. I follow you on Twitter." I smiled and nodded. I didn't know what to say. Apparently, he didn't either as he just stood there, in the cramped deli, waiting for me to respond.

"Cool, thanks for following me." I meant it in a digital sense. I waved goodbye, grabbed my food, and left. To this day, it remains the oddest fan interaction I've ever had.

A month later, I channeled my neuroses into positive action

and called in every favor I could to produce a star-studded comedy and music benefit show at Irving Plaza for the Doctors Without Borders Ebola relief efforts in West Africa. We had incredible performers such as Regina Spektor, Jim Gaffigan, Janeane Garofalo, David Cross, Fred Armisen, Jessica Williams, Ira Glass, and Ted Leo on the bill, and we managed to raise $15,000 for the organization. I even invited Dr. Adalja to conduct a Q and A in between performances, while the musical acts were setting up. Somehow, according to friends in the audience, my new infectious-disease doctor friend who'd never been onstage before stole the show.

A year later Dr. Adalja even consulted on a script I wrote inspired by the Doctors Without Borders doctor Craig Spencer, who inadvertently brought Ebola to New York City and briefly became a tabloid sensation. Looking back on that news story, it feels more like an ominous foreshadowing of what was to come than a premise for a feature-length comedy.

"What's a good name for a fake but real-seeming Ebola-like infectious disease that also could be an acronym for an emasculated man's name?" I inquired.

"Maybe something that starts with a C for a coronavirus. Pretty soon they're going to be all the rage," Dr. Adalja actually said, in 2015. And thus, my ill-fated infectious disease rom-comedy *21 Days of CARL* (an acronym for coronavirus-associated reticular lymphopenia) was born. The plot centered on a woman who was forced into quarantine after a one-night stand with a journalist who had just returned from a hot zone. It was a little like *Bridget Jones's Diary* meets *Contagion,* and the only reason I bring it up is to give you a sense of what an infectious-disease-obsessed nut I am and what state of mind I was in when I was deciding whether or not to do that cross-country college gig at the onset of a global pandemic.

When I called Dr. Adalja to gauge his thoughts, he informed me that this coronavirus didn't appear as deadly as SARS or MERS and probably wouldn't kill me even if I got it (cool, cool, cool). It also wasn't YET a pandemic, so the chances of being exposed to it were slim. I deliberated on it for a few days and then hesitantly made up my mind.

I was going to do the show.

At 1:20 a.m. on February 7, 2020, I put on an N95 mask I had been saving for a rainy day and boarded a flight out of LAX, connecting in Chicago to Albany, New York. By the time I landed in Albany, it was snowing pretty intensely. I remember the snow so vividly because I had forgotten that it was winter on the East Coast and I was wearing sandals. A student at the university picked me up from the airport and drove me to the hotel in town. I was pretty delirious by that point. I had taken two flights to get to the show on time, and after over eleven hours of flying, I was exhausted. When I finally got to my hotel room around two p.m., I set my alarm to five p.m., collapsed on the bed, and immediately fell into a deep sleep.

I woke up a few hours later to multiple missed calls from my agent. What was going on? When I called her back, she informed me that due to the unexpected snowstorm, the university was canceling our show, *and* not paying us the money we were owed.

Excuse me? I didn't even know that was an option.

"Can they do that?" I asked in a still-half-asleep stupor. My agent sighed. Apparently, a force majeure clause in the contract enabled them to cancel the show without having to compensate "the talent." She was just as annoyed as I was, and she assured me that she would do her best to get the money, but legally speaking, there was no guarantee. I was livid, not just at the potential loss of income but also by the principle of it all. We have so few industry protections as comedians.

I was so frustrated in that moment, primarily at the university with a $364 million endowment attempting not to compensate comedians who flew across the country to work there. I also still really wanted to get paid.

I wondered aloud to my agent, "Can we do the show off campus?"

"Where are you thinking?"

"Anywhere? A bar? A restaurant? A bookstore? Literally anywhere. I just want to get paid." Which isn't always the best motivation going into a live show, but at that point, I didn't really care.

A few minutes later, my agent called back, "There's a pizza place. . . ."

"I'm in."

"It doesn't have a stage."

"Fine."

"Or much light."

"Great."

"They also don't have a sound system, but they might be able to get a small speaker and a mic."

"Now you're talking!"

"And it will be open to the public, so I imagine there will be other people in there, probably eating during the show."

"Sounds like my target demo. Let's do it!"

"All right, I'll let you know what they say."

My agent hung up the phone and my enthusiasm drained. What was I getting myself into? Whatever you've read about ideal conditions for stand-up comedy to work—a well-lit stage with a dimly lit room, low ceilings, a captive audience, no threat of an airborne infectious virus—this was not that. It quickly dawned on me that my hour show that I had worked on for over a year and a half was now going to be performed in a pizza shop in a college town in the middle of a blizzard AND an emerging pandemic. Stand-up comedy is so humbling.

Naturally, I wasn't in the best mood that night (three hours of sleep will do that to you), but I was still getting paid to do what I love, so I tried to focus on that. When I arrived at the pizza place, I realized there was no way I would be able to perform my solo show in a noisy restaurant with no stage, lighting, or sound system. The show was also pretty political and dark and maybe not the best fit for an Upstate New York bar crowd. I asked the student organizers if a shorter, more conventional stand-up set might work better in this context, and they gave me the go-ahead to do that instead. I cut my show in half and ended up doing a condensed version of it with some other, more apolitical, bar-friendly jokes sprinkled in. The set went okay, about as well as one can expect a set to go, on very little sleep and in a room with poor sound and bright lighting and an audience more interested in eating pizza than in getting ambushed into watching a free comedy show.

After the show, the student organizers thanked me and the other comic on the bill for going with the flow and putting on the show. He and I laughed about it as we walked back to our hotel through the icy blizzard (I was still wearing sandals).

"At least we both got ten thousand dollars out of it," he chuckled as he retreated to his hotel room. I forced myself to smile as I waved goodbye.

I got paid $6,000.*

I flew back to Los Angeles and promptly started isolating and prepping for the end of the world (by loading up on canned soup and by freaking out my live-in boyfriend, Josh, enough to start isolating with me). I didn't think much about the show until five days later, when I received this lovely email (which I've condensed for clarity).

On Thursday, February 13, 2020, 11:40 AM, Cathy [**Redacted**] <cathy.[**redacted**]@icloud.com> wrote:

Hi Jena,

I'm the mom of one of the student producers of [redacted]. I flew out from California last Friday to see the show that my daughter and her classmates had been working so hard on for the past several months. . . .

Everyone in that room deserved so much more than you gave them. I simply don't understand why you went the route you did, barely phoning in a snide, lackluster performance rather than trying to make the best of a frustrating situation for everyone involved. Imagine how the students felt when the show they had so carefully coordinated and rehearsed was canceled at the last minute. You were not the only one who had to deal with disappointment. . . .

---

*$6,000 is $4,500 after agent (10 percent of gross), manager (10 percent of gross), and lawyer (5 percent of gross) fees, $3,500 when you factor in flights and cars to the airports, and then you have to pay taxes (roughly 30 percent), for a net total of $2,400 . . . if you don't eat.

They say a person's true character is revealed in times of adversity—yeah, well.

—Cathy

Sent from Yahoo Mail for iPhone

Why are they always named Cathy? I wish I could have ignored her letter and not included it in this book, but I'm still clearly not over it. I RISKED MY LIFE FOR THOSE KIDS. Okay, maybe that's a hair dramatic. I RISKED MY LIFE FOR THAT ($2,400 NET REVENUE) PAYCHECK! Looking back on the letter now, it is pretty funny that Cathy referred to our impromptu comedy show in a pizza place as "times of adversity," given what we all had coming down the pipeline a month later. But in the moment, her letter cut deep, maybe because a small part of me agreed with her. Even in the least optimal conditions and most flustered headspace, I still wanted to put on a good show. It also gave me renewed empathy for schoolteachers. If one mom's critical letter could ruin my week, I could only imagine how frustrating it must be for teachers, who probably have to field critical feedback from over-involved helicopter parents every day.

I didn't know how to respond, which means I probably shouldn't have responded. In general, it's never a good idea to put anything in print that you might regret, but I was truly incensed. I didn't intentionally phone in my set; I just didn't know how to retool an hour show in a moment's notice in a venue where I knew it wouldn't work. Should I have dusted off more decade-old sex jokes and done them instead? Absolutely! But hindsight is 20/20, and also pandering to what I know a crowd will want really isn't my style.*

I showed the email to my beloved partner, Josh, who is also a touring performer, hoping that he would talk me down from a ledge, which he always does. Instead he was pissed off for me.

"They weren't going to pay you?!"

"I know!"

"And they tried to cancel the show?"

"Yep."

"And YOU saved it by moving it to another venue at the last minute?"

"I guess I *did* save the show, now that I think about it...."

"And this random lady is mad at you?"

"Yes! Cathy. She is quite random."

"That's so annoying!"

"I know!"

Josh giggled. "Okay.... Here's what you should write...."

Just so you know, I don't typically ask my incredibly wonderful now-husband (we got married in September 2021—I guess that's one good thing to come out of the pandemic) to help me navigate complex tasks like responding to angry emails, but the next line out of his mouth genuinely made me laugh in a moment when I really needed to (he's actually very funny for a musician). It was maybe a little too harsh to write to a stranger on the internet, but we're all works in progress and besides, she did start it. Plus, this was the early days of the pandemic, and I was a little out of sorts and maybe not on my best behavior. So per Josh's snarky suggestion, I wrote her back.

---

* If only it were, I'd be so much more successful now.

Thanks for the note, Cathy! I can see why your daughter chose
to go to college across the country.

Sent from Yahoo Mail for iPhone

Unsurprisingly, I never heard from Cathy again.

Looking back now, if I could have done things differently—
besides request that I be paid up front or not fly across the country
at the onset of a global pandemic in the first place—I would have
performed my entire hour-long show as I had originally written
it. Because it would end up being one of the last opportunities I
would ever get to perform that show, which I had been working
on for so long and hoped to tour and eventually tape. Since the
show was so political and timely, the pandemic and the passage
of time rendered it obsolete. It would also be one of the last times
that I would get to perform stand-up comedy for eighteen months,
something that I had done consistently, at least once a week, for
fourteen years.

And although an hour of me talking about mass shootings,
white supremacy, and violence against women in a pizza joint
probably would have gone over even worse than my condensed set
of one-liners, I bet poor Cathy would have hated it, and that would
have been reason enough for me!

On Making It

One afternoon in the summer of 2015, I was working out of the edit bay at *The Daily Show with Jon Stewart* when Jon strolled into our office to say hi. Normally, particularly on a show day, Jon would have been too busy working nonstop to casually shoot the shit with us. But in those last few weeks of his historic, sixteen-year-run, the vibe was different. At one point, someone asked him, "When did you know you made it?" Jon thought for a moment, and then responded, "I still don't."

Everyone laughed, except for me. "I remember the low points in my career," Jon continued. "Like when my MTV show got canceled and how I thought I might never work again. I remember when I performed stand-up on *Letterman* for the first time, which had always been a huge career goal of mine, and how afterward, I went back to my small, rat-infested apartment and realized that nothing had changed. I was still a struggling stand-up comic and I was still five-eight."

Again, everyone laughed except for me, who thought he was closer to five-seven.*

It was an eye-opening moment, and a real window into the psyche of a stand-up comedian. However you define success—financial, critical, cultural, etc.—Jon's tenure at *The Daily Show* was all of the above. After twenty-two Emmys (he was an executive producer on Colbert's show, too!) and too many other achievements to count, if even Jon fucking Stewart didn't truly believe that he had "made it" in the entertainment industry, what hope did the rest of us have?

When I was a young improviser in Chicago, I was dating a fellow improviser and I remember thinking that he had "made it," because at that time, I thought "making it" was just being able to do what you love and not go broke in the process. He was working part-time in retail to pay the bills, but it meant he got to perform improv every night on various shows around Chicago. I had a well-paying job in consulting that I hated because it took me out of the city during the week. If only I could just be in town more often so that I could do improv more often . . . then maybe I too could "make it."

When I left that job and that guy and started doing stand-up, my benchmark for what constituted "making it" shifted. Chicago comics who are household names now (Kumail Nanjiani, Hannibal Buress) were actually getting paid to perform, and I decided then that getting paid for your work was *really* "making it." If only I could just get paid to do stand-up,† I thought. *That* would be "making it."

---

* Jk, I love you, Jon!

† Little did I know back then that fifteen years later, I would still not be making a living wage from stand-up alone.

When I finally booked my first paid gig at Zanies Comedy Club in Chicago in 2007, I thought I was well on my way to "making it"—that is, until I got the check a few weeks later in the mail and saw that my earnings for a ten-minute spot of my best material that took me months to generate amounted to $13.07, after taxes. I kept that check in my desk drawer and never cashed it, less for sentimental reasons than because it would have cost me more to take it to a bank.* Turns out, "getting paid" to do stand-up comedy doesn't really constitute making it, because the majority of people who do stand-up barely make enough money to consistently cover their rent. Even the best comedians in Chicago weren't able to make a living wage purely on stand-up. If I reallllly wanted to make it, I would have to move to New York.

When I finally moved to New York two years later, I discovered that even getting to do paid stand-up spots every night (mostly paid in drink tickets) wouldn't be enough to cover my rent, which was three times what it had been in Chicago. I also noticed that so many comics I admired (like Morgan Murphy and Ali Waller) were writing for late-night shows. They weren't just getting paid to do comedy, they were making a really good living doing it, and that became my new benchmark. If only I had a writing job, where I could pay my rent and have health insurance, *then* I'd *really* be living the dream.

A few years later I finally got that dream late-night writing job, and to my surprise, it wasn't all it was cracked up to be. I was having a hard time getting sketches on the show and was in constant fear that I might get fired at any minute (we were on thirteen-week contracts, so the fear wasn't in my head). If only I

---

* Time is money, people!

could make a living writing for myself, then THAT would actually be "making it."

The goalposts were always shifting, even after my first late-night stand-up set on *Conan* and my second, and my first stand-up special and then my Adult Swim show. They were career highlights, for sure, but nothing ever really felt like a game changer. But then this past year came the one thing that kinda sorta did: an Oscar nomination.

I was quarantined in Los Angeles when I learned that I had just been nominated for Best Adapted Screenplay in 2021 as part of the writing team on *Borat: Subsequent Moviefilm: Delivery of Prodigious Bribe to American Regime for Make Benefit Once Glorious Nation of Kazakhstan*. There is so much I want to say about working on that fever dream of a project, but I am sworn to secrecy by an ironclad NDA and an allegiance to a boss who trusted me enough to put a menstrual-blood dance and a scene at a pregnancy crisis center in his broad studio comedy. I was in such shock that our movie even got made and that no one got killed in the process of making it (although Sacha did come close during that gun rally in Washington State) that when I first heard we were nominated, my reaction was muted. I stared at my phone as I watched countless texts from close friends, estranged exes, and everyone in between roll in to offer congratulations on such a crowning career achievement. Instantly, I recalled that conversation with Jon and wondered if this was really it. Had I finally "made it"? And if so, why didn't I feel like it? Was it due to the fact that after fifteen years of being beaten down by an industry that rarely loves you back, I was too tired to feel anything?

Regardless, I knew this was a once-in-a-lifetime opportunity, particularly for a comedian, since comedies rarely get nominated, and if I wasn't feeling pure, unbridled excitement about it, I was just going to have to fake it. I decided I would even lean in to the *hoopla* (that's not the word) and go to every pre-Oscar event I was invited to! Turns out that in the midst of a global pandemic, there was only one: a socially distanced awards show gifting suite. Great, whatever that is, sign me up!

If you've never heard of gifting suites, aka "luxury lounges," these ostentatious displays of late-stage capitalism are a staple of every Hollywood award season, which I believe begins in mid-January and runs through . . . December?[*] Don't quote me. A more desperate cousin of the awards show gift bag, the Hollywood gifting suite dates back to 1994, when a former Grammy producer hatched a scheme to convince celebrities to show up to event rehearsals on time. "[Karen] Wood quickly realized that stuffing the greenroom with freebies that the celebrities might be interested in helped with their punctuality."[†] Moral of the story: celebrities are like little children. You have to give them gifts if you want them to do things.

I had been given a plus one, so I roped in a dear friend to join me. The moment we arrived, the event's organizer came over to greet us, because who else was she going to talk to? We were the only people there. I scanned the patio for any familiar face, but the space was virtually empty except for a handful of bored staffers, a few photographers, and about a dozen small business owners, each eyeing us as they hovered over their merch tables

---

[*] It seems as if someone is always being congratulated for something in Hollywood . . . like how Christmas is always being celebrated in some parts of the South, "award season" is a perennial season in Hollywood.

[†] Celia Walden, "There's No Such Thing as a Free Cannabis Truffle: Inside Hollywood's Gift Bag Economy," *Telegraph*, February 19, 2019.

full of random candles and non-FDA-approved vitamins, eager to hawk their wares. It turns out, almost all of the entrepreneurs were moms who had "quit" their jobs (i.e., or more likely been pushed out of the workforce for being human women with kids, but that's another essay entirely) to start their own businesses and who were hoping to use this event to gain brand visibility by being photographed with Oscar nominees. It suddenly dawned on me that perhaps it was me, and not the junk these women were giving away, that was actually the product. Did *this* mean I'd made it?

I didn't totally register that I was going to THE ACTUAL OSCARS until a day before the event, when I still had no idea what I was going to wear. Yes, that last sentence just set my feminist antennas on fire, but the Oscars are one of the most fashion-y events in my industry and since I am a human woman, not a male comic, I couldn't just roll up in jeans and a black T-shirt. Plus, I had been wearing sweatpants every day for the past year—what better time to change it up a little? But there was one problem: I have no fashion sense. A lot of comics don't. I'm not gonna pull a *Fashion Police* Joan Rivers (may she rest in peace) and name-drag any unfashionable funny people down with me, but just google-image your favorite comic and "red carpet" and you'll see what I mean (with one exception being the inimitable Patti Harrison: her fashion sense is impeccable).

Luckily, my brilliant friend, stylist Kat Typaldos, ran all around Los Angeles with me to find the perfect outfit to wear on the red carpet and the perfect jewelry (on loan) to match. I glided through the pre-Oscar prep following her lead, amazed by how much thought and effort went into every single detail.

The show itself was surreal, but it also felt like a TV taping, which it technically was. It was cool to be there, especially knowing that it was probably the only Oscars that would take place at a train station in downtown L.A. in the middle of a global pandemic. But also my dress was way too tight to walk in, and because we were still in the early post–first wave of the pandemic days, there was very little socializing. At one point, when my friends left to smoke a cigarette, I checked Instagram (it's my addiction that I'm trying to kick) and saw that the white dress I'd somehow managed to stuff myself into had already gone viral (fashion world viral). A blogger had established that there was a "white dress trend" at the 2021 Oscars and I was apparently part of it. Cool? I've never been part of any online trend, let alone a fashion one, and now my face and BODY were all over the internet. In my decade and a half as a comic, nothing I have actually accomplished has gotten as much traction in such a short amount of time as that one photo of me in a too-tight white dress. It's kind of depressing when you think about it, but also . . . did *THIS* mean I'd made it?

It wasn't until we were ushered into the train station auditorium at the start of the show that I actually thought, *Holy shit: maybe I REALLY HAVE MADE IT!* Here I was, in a room full of insanely talented artists and filmmakers from around the world who had achieved a level of success my younger self (or me, two years earlier) would never even have dreamed of, about to watch the freaking Oscars that I was also IN. It was an incredible feeling, and it lasted about twenty minutes, up until the moment that the winner in our category was announced and—spoiler alert—it wasn't us! I didn't actually think we were going to win, but I also didn't realize how much less fun the Oscars can be (not that I have anything to compare it to) when you don't win.

After the first act, we were corralled out of the awards show and into a lounge area, where those grasping their golden statues were separated from the rest of the pack and bum-rushed by swarms of reporters and hangers-on, while everyone else was quickly cast aside. Throughout the rest of the evening, as more winners filtered out of the show and into the lounge, it was kind of funny to watch Hollywood's classiest night descend into what can only be described as an elevated version of a high school cafeteria, with the Oscar winners being the popular kids and the rest of us wondering if we'd ever work again. Nothing encapsulates the experience of being in entertainment more than being at the apex of your career and still feeling like you are less than someone else.

But looking back, what I remember most about the whole Oscar experience wasn't anything that happened inside the venue. It was the feeling I had as I was getting ready at home with my friends. My stylist friend Kat and three of my other friends, Anu, Bella, and Molly, were there with me, advising me on everything from which dress to wear (Kat brought options) to how to stand for the press photos (apparently it's a science!). We were laughing and drinking champagne and just taking in the insanity. At one point, I thought about all the other milestones I had been through with each of them: Molly is an old friend from college and one of the smartest people I know. She was with me on election night 2016, when I bombed on *Colbert*. Anu and Bella are insanely talented directors, close friends, and collaborators, both of whom I've been lucky enough to work with on various projects. (Anu directed the first episode of my first television show, *Soft Focus*, and Bella was who I turned to at the beginning of the pandemic, when the world shut down and my stand-up tour was canceled and I still had to find a way to make money. The two of us put our heads together and made a weird but cute pandemic web series, called

The Joy of Quarantine, which is on YouTube if you're ever curious to learn how not to cook a chicken.)

I know it sounds cheesy, but while getting ready for the show, I felt like a bride hanging out with her bridesmaids on her wedding day, or at least how I imagine that might feel*: giddy and excited and maybe a little tipsy, because champagne on an empty stomach will do that to you. When it was time to leave, my friends pushed me and Josh out the door with cheers and "Good lucks!" as I piled myself and my too-tight white vintage Mugler (RIP Thierry) gown into a chauffeured car (courtesy of the producers) with Josh dressed in black alongside me. We really did look like a bride and groom (he actually married me in that same tux a few months later). As Josh and I headed to the show, I felt so grateful: both for the people in my life and the work that I had gotten to do that brought me to that moment. I didn't know what would happen next, and I still didn't know what "making it" meant, but I knew right then—however long it lasted—that this was as close as it gets.

---

*I didn't have bridesmaids at my wedding and would never subject my closest friends to that.

Acknowledgments

So many people have helped in the conception, gestation, and delivery of this book, I don't even know where to begin expressing my gratitude. I'll start by thanking my lit agent, Robert Guinsler, who convinced me that we might be able to sell a series of essays off a satirical tweet about Brock Turner that too many people thought was real. Thanks to Nick Ciani and the team at One Signal, who took a chance on someone whose essay writing, prior to this book, rarely exceeded 140 characters. Thanks to Carolyn Murnick for being a most trusted set of eyeballs and for helping me break through my writer's block. Thanks to all of my dear friends, colleagues, and comedy witches who have inspired and supported me over the years, including Elna Baker, Anu Valia, Jessica Delfino, Nur El Shami Goldstein, Rachel Pikelny, Nell Constantinople, David Rood-Ojalvo, Abby Melone, Molly Smith, Jessica Bennett, Amanda McCall, Lucia Aniello and the WHENies, Patti Harrison, Atsuko Okatsuka, Naomi Ekperigin, J.C. Coccoli, Eliza Skinner, Sarah Schaefer, Francesca Fiorentini, Adira Amram,

Acknowledgments

Sarah Watson, Elaine Malcolmson, Phoebe Bourke, Tiff Stevenson, Jacqueline Novak, Joyelle Johnson, Morgan Murphy, Reggie Watts, Bob Odenkirk, Alison Camillo, Sam Bee, Tim Greenberg, Wyatt Cenac, Sacha Baron Cohen, Ant Hines, Ashley and Larry Underwood, Marla Guttman, Bella Monticelli, Whitney Cummings, Benj Pasek, Mehran Khaghani, Noam Dworman and Estee Adoram, Steve Lock, Deborah Campbell, Audrey Milstein, Matt Harrigan, Mike Lazzo, Paige Boudreaux, Marco Brezas, Neil McDonald, Carolyn Lehman and the team at AMC, Seth Herzog, Merrill Markoe, Tracey Jackson, Lou Wallach, Nell Scovell, Allison Bills, Scott Illingsworth and the cast and crew of *The Refugee Girls' Revue*, Teresa Spizzirri, Ruth Gamble, Fawzia Mirza, Dave Hill, Marc Rubin, Dr. Amesh Adalja, Jake Salyers, Kaila Kuban, Francine and Julie Hermelin, Jon Philpot, Jeannie and Jim Gaffigan, Julia Pishko, Kat Typaldos, Jason Selvig and Davram Steifler, and so many others. Thanks to Professor Micaela di Leonardo, who taught me how to see the world with a (feminist Marxist) anthropologist's eye and to my lawyer, Josh Sandler, who has saved my ass literally and figuratively so many times. Thank you Jon Stewart, for being a mentor in every sense of the word and for teaching me how to make anything funny. Thanks to Heidi Feigin, Bjorn Wentlandt, Ali Benmohamed, Talia Myers, and the team at UTA, and to Sam Srinivasan. Thanks to J.P. Buck and Conan O'Brien for believing in and amplifying my stand-up comedy when no other late-night shows would. Thanks to Stephen Colbert for your generosity and kindness and for continuing to have me on, despite the words that come out of my mouth. Thanks to Austin Nelson, for all of your gorgeous photos, including the one on this cover. Thanks to Seth Olenick and Mindy Tucker, and to Hillary Fitzgerald Campbell for normalizing my obsession with

Acknowledgments

true crime. Thanks to Larry, Mary, and Lanie Epstein—you're the best in-laws a person could hope for! Thanks to my mom, Iris, who has been telling me "you should write a book" since I started crowning, and to my dad, Robert, who supported my comedy before it was cool and nurtured my most morose comedic impulses for as long as I can remember. Thanks to Dara, who is probably why I am a comedian, and thanks to Josh, my love, who makes me laugh every day, who gave me the space to write this book while we were trapped at home during a global pandemic and the encouragement to stick with it after we got vaccinated. Last but not least, thank you Potato, for not barking too much to distract me from my work and for not peeing on the printer, after that one time you peed on the printer.

About the Author

Jena Friedman is an Oscar-nominated writer, director, and comedian. She is the host of the comedic true-crime series *Indefensible* on AMC Plus and the creator of *Soft Focus* on Adult Swim. Friedman has been published in the *New Yorker* and has appeared on such programs as *The Late Show with Stephen Colbert*, *Conan* on TBS, and *The Nightly Show with Larry Wilmore* and in the Sundance hit movie *Palm Springs*. Behind the scenes, she has field produced for *The Daily Show with Jon Stewart* and has written for *Late Show with David Letterman*, *The Conners* on ABC, and *Borat Subsequent Moviefilm*.